Language Teaching and the Microcomputer

For Oksana

Language Teaching and The Microcomputer

Rex Last

Basil Blackwell

© Rex Last 1984

First published 1984
Basil Blackwell Limited
108 Cowley Road, Oxford OX4 1JF, England

British Library Cataloguing in Publication Data

Last, R.W.
   Language teaching and the microcomputer.
   1. Language and languages – Computer assisted instruction
   I. Title
   407'.8   P53

   ISBN 0-631-13413-1

Typesetting by Katerprint Limited, Oxford
Printed in Great Britain by T J Press, Padstow.

Contents

Foreword

In the following pages, you will find a personal and informal account of the present state of the art of computer-assisted language learning, set in the context of the history of computer applications in language and literature.

This book is designed to meet the needs of teachers anxious to make some sense of the new microtechnology as it relates to the acquisition of language skills. By 'language' I do not simply mean 'modern languages': what follows is of equal relevance for the English, EFL and indeed Classics teacher, and there is, I hope, more than a little of interest for those teaching other disciplines across the curriculum.

The objective has been to identify and describe the principal trends and issues rather than to analyse in detail every last research project there has ever been in this field. Jargon and buzz-words are explained as the text proceeds, but a couple of acronyms require instant attention: CAL is Computer-Assisted Learning, and the rather unlovely CALL (which has invited unwarranted observations about CALL-persons and the like) breaks down to Computer-Assisted Language Learning. Not to be outdone, the Americans prefer CAI (Computer-Aided Instruction) and CALI (Computer-Aided Language Instruction) respectively. This book studiously avoids the largely lexical debate about the precise differences between instruction and learning in this field.

It also avoids footnotes, since the interested reader can rapidly gain access to all the important and relevant material via the bibliographical appendix. As one American article aptly puts it: 'The literature on CAI is vast but repetitive. . .'

and 'the record of actual use of CAI has also been spotty.' I have endeavoured not to be too repetitive nor too spotty, but apologise in advance for any sins of commission or omission.

Thanks are especially due to the following for their assistance, intentional or otherwise: Ned Davison, Graham Davies, Derek Lewis, Oksana Last, and also the many institutions who kindly invited me to address them on this subject, thereby allowing me to test out some of the material contained in this book in field conditions.

Introduction

As I was putting this book together, I could almost hear the collective groan rising up from staff and common rooms throughout the land: Surely not *another* breezy little introduction to the mighty micro, more pressure on us to dabble in expensive, irrelevant and time-consuming technology at a time when the teacher is struggling simply to survive in an increasingly harsh and hostile world and is hard put to find the price of a box of chalk, let alone a roomful of micros.

Such a reaction is, to put it mildly, more than understandable, particularly at a time of much general political tub-thumping about the need to embrace the chip or perish, to espouse what is vaguely dubbed 'information technology', without the well-meaning generalities having yet been satisfactorily translated into positive action on the ground (with a few laudable exceptions). Computers are now supposed to be operating across the curriculum, but one micro to a thousand pupils is not likely to achieve this end for a very long time. Hence it is not to be wondered at that the school of criticism which cheerfully asserted 'I have not read *Lady Chatterley's Lover* but I think it should be banned' is alive and well among the anti-computer lobbyists.

There is no escaping the fact that CALL is new and, like all new things, treated by one camp with deep suspicion, and by a handful of enthusiasts with over-optimistic glee. It has been condemned on the one hand as impersonal and pedagogically unsound, and praised to the skies on the other as ushering in a new era of open, interactive and creative learning. As usual the truth lies somewhere in between, and it is my purpose to determine precisely where the truth is to be located.

This book does not set out to present, from the cushioned comfort of my academic ivory tower, an evangelistic eulogy of the micro which seeks to lay down the law as to how this new technological miracle must be used by the hard-pressed teacher to resolve all his problems. What follows is based on practical experience of CALL, not only at university level, but with teachers' groups and a research project investigating the feasibility and desirability of extending the role of the computer in modern language teaching in Scottish schools.

I hope I am as aware as most educators of the fact that teaching requirements depend upon all manner of constraints such as time, objectives, group size, resources available, personal inclination, and so forth, and that technological aids – from blackboard to videodisc via computer – may or may not be either desirable or, indeed, available, as solutions to particular problems within an overall teaching objective. In the last analysis, I tend to the view that it does not matter a great deal what the technique, methodology or theoretical precepts of the teacher are, the central issue is the personality and qualities of the teacher.

I am aware that many readers will have shared the embarrassing experience of having been a material witness at a so-called 'demonstration' of CALL by an enthusiastic microphile who has had his machine for a fortnight or so, and who has mastered the first few pages of the handbook. The demonstration inevitably goes hopelessly wrong, leaving all concerned (save for the demonstrator) even more convinced than ever that computers and language teaching have nothing at all to do with one another. Fortunately, there has been considerable progress over the past few years in CALL, and the days of the well-meaning amateur are all but over. A really professional approach from a number of research teams has generated CALL material of genuinely high quality and great potential.

However, it must be said that good-quality courseware for

language teaching (and indeed for many other disciplines) is still in very short supply. The reasons behind this are clear: the art of CALL is relatively new, and, as this book hopes to demonstrate, the acquisition of the relevant skills for the creation of CALL courseware is a far from trivial business.

If the assumption about CALL being the province of amateurs is misguided, so too is the view I have often heard advanced by the computerphobes, namely, that CALL is the creature of one particular (and outdated) theoretical approach to the business of language teaching. It is a common misconception – and it *is* a total misconception – that computer-assisted learning is identical to programmed learning. The fact that the one grew out of the other does not mean that the two are indissolubly bound now any more than they logically were in the halcyon days when the technological approach to the resolution of educational problems seemed set to provide the panacea.

The spectator at a performance of a less than perfect musical work, you will recall, was advised not to shoot the pianist; rejecting the computer on the grounds that it is only programmed learning writ large would be rather like counselling the selfsame spectator to shoot the piano.

As I hope to demonstrate, the computer can do far more in CALL than silently ape the 'tutorial' mode of question-and-answer instruction, although even that approach is not to be despised if properly applied in due moderation and in the appropriate context.

Stating the problem the other way round, it is equally untrue that the computer – or, indeed, the language laboratory before it – forces the teacher to modify his or her pedagogical approach to suit the hardware. Bad teaching practices which derived from an unimaginative application of the language laboratory will equally be found among the CALL programs currently available – and there are some pretty ghastly examples of how not to program; but it is also true that there are some less than successful teaching methods around which use nothing more technological than a piece of chalk and a blackboard. It is a pity that many defenders and attackers of particular approaches to teaching and learning do not employ the same rigorous logic in their own argumentation that they claim to inculcate in their pupils by means of their favourite teaching methods.

One of the key choices that has to be made about microtechnology in language teaching is not necessarily how best to use it, but whether it is relevant to employ it at all in the particular circumstances of a given teacher. However, it is surely preferable for those who decide against employing the micro to base their choice on an informed evaluation of the subject rather than on a gut reaction to the generalised and distorted picture of the newly-dawned golden age of the micro presented by the mass media, the computing comics, the people selling micros in an overcrowded and highly competitive market, and the ill-informed enthusiasms or Luddite prejudices of some educationalists.

My aim is quite modest: to provide the interested and probably sceptical language teacher – whose store cupboards are littered with discarded hardware from past excursions into educational technology – with a practical guide to the chequered history and intriguing present of the relationship between computer and linguist. An account is offered of how the two became involved with one another and how a few literary scholars somewhat unexpectedly became caught up in computing; the lessons of early and subsequent research are explored; a case history is used to demonstrate the principal theoretical and practical problems raised by CALL; and this is followed by a survey of how the micro is currently being employed in language teaching. The variety of applications is quite substantial, a real tribute to the ingenuity of the enthusiasts.

Some of this book, which is ostensibly concerned with CALL, is devoted to a consideration of the history of computer applications in language and literature, and the reader impatient to explore first the practicalities of CALL is invited to skip Chapter 2 if needs be, simply glancing at the list of lessons from the past at the end of the chapter. However, the reader should bear in mind that it is vital not only to set CALL in its historical context, but also to examine and become acquainted with the lessons to be learned from past excursions by the computer into natural language. Without a knowledge of the early experiments and the developments that followed, the danger exists that the CALL enthusiast will have to learn these lessons all over again in his or her present work.

Hence the historical chapter is not an academic indulgence; it forms the proper foundation for present and future progress in the field of CALL and makes fascinating reading in its own right. The core of the book is Chapter 7, which details current CALL practice and seeks to draw a number of conclusions about the proper implementation of CALL.

One additional factor for the impatient reader to consider is the fact that the relative paucity of good-quality ready-made CALL software on the market is due neither to ineptitude nor sloth on the part of the package writers: as indicated earlier, all new techniques in educational technology demand a certain irreducible amount of time for their acquisition and development, and soundly-tested routines based on a proper understanding of all the issues involved are the only basis for real progress. It took television a decade or more to come of age as an educational tool and if we date the real onset of CALL on the microcomputer to, say, the beginning of this decade, the pace of progress on CALL has been far from slothful, given the magnitude of the issues involved and the new techniques to be mastered.

1

Stating the problem

Murphy's First Law of Computing states that, in order to gain expertise in any one aspect of the subject, it is first necessary to be conversant with every other aspect of the subject, including the one which is currently being mastered. That seems hardly an encouraging way to start a book which seeks at least to inform and at best to enthuse language teachers about the role of the computer in language learning, but it is very important that the reader should not set off with any preconceptions about how easy computing is supposed to be, and the fact that the problems in learning computing and a language have not a little in common at least points to some affinities between the two disciplines. Grammar and syntax are terms to be found in both areas, and the common ground is such that, in my view, the languages expert is particularly well adapted to becoming a computer programmer, much better so than the average scientist.

We are all being bombarded with glossy advertisements commending the merits of Brand X Micro, which proclaim how simple it is to master the silicon chip and program the machine using BASIC, which – to paraphrase more than one recent advert – 'is essentially just plain English.' If, to quote one dialect of BASIC, what follows is just plain English, then I would rather be spared the sight of complicated English:

LET TOT$=MSK('zz9.99',VAL(TOT$)+T)

Language teachers quite understandably get annoyed when they are told that it is child's play to learn a language and to pick up a smattering of this or that tongue without the intervention of an instructor, particularly when outsiders confuse the talent to mop up, sponge-like, a working knowledge of a language with the quite distinct and difficult accomplishment of mastering a language (and culture) in all its intricacies and ramifications. And I am quite surprised that computer folk for their part have not risen up as one person in protest at the not dissimilar extravagant claims of those whose obvious principal motivation is to sell the maximum number of micros to the largest number of customers in the shortest possible time. It is not, repeat not, child's play to master the micro. What is easy, given the packages presently available, is to use the micro for specific applications, whether they be games, word processors, database management systems, spreadsheets or the rest.

Real computing, like natural languages, is by no means a simple discipline to master: the rather awful programming language available on most micros called BASIC enables you to make a start, but it is only a *Beginners'* All-purpose Symbolic Instruction Code, and even its structured variants do not and cannot aim to provide the aspirant programmer with anything approaching a full command and knowledge of the micro, although the best BASICs, like that on the BBC micro, come close to offering a complete and satisfactory approach to many microcomputing applications.

Besides, it is not just a matter of learning how to 'program' a computer skilfully and efficiently. There are other issues demanding quite different skills which also have to be resolved: problems like the educational principles underlying the programs you are devising have to be considered, as too does the question of the man–machine interface (to borrow the jargon), or 'software psychology', as it is called. More of that unlikely-sounding phrase later. Computing is one area in which the cheerful amateurism of the British can and usually does produce disastrous results.

Equally, it is important to come to terms with what the computer can and cannot do, if its potential is to be properly exploited in the achievement of educational ends. The temptation to tailor educational practice to meet the con-straints of the hardware must be avoided; some of the drill and practice routines devised in the past for the language laboratory certainly fall into the category of exercises being designed round the technology, and have led to less than satisfactory results for both teacher and learner.

The computer can function in certain areas much better than in others, for example, in analysing rather than synthesising; and the difficulties encountered by those working in the area of artificial intelligence and expert systems underline the painfully slow progress being made in seeking to create programs which simulate the way in which human beings think.

To strike another pessimistic note: not surprisingly, many teachers, once bitten by the language laboratory, fight very shy of the cheerful cries of the enthusiasts on the computer band-wagon, not least because the skills that can be tested appear to have a sinister ring of the oldfashioned about them (and there is, as linguists know, nothing more damning than to be numbered among the oldfashioned).

In the case of the language laboratory, the irony of the present situation is that the whole notion of language laboratories has fallen into considerable disfavour at the very time when a new generation of microprocessor-controlled laboratories has come on the market. There is now the medium-term prospect of what might be termed 'total learning stations', combining the features of language labora-tory with a cassette recorder under full computer control (of which more later), video viewing position, high-speed random access interactive video, a computer terminal for CALL work, and a wide variety of other functions.

As in the past, the language teacher has a real prospect of benefit from new technology only if it has a broad base in the popular mass market (as with cassette audio and video recorders, and now with the micro). In addition, the language teacher is no longer likely to buy an 'empty box', a pretty new technological toy, without good quality software and courseware to make it work efficiently and profitably in the classroom.

If you have not given up in despair by this time, let me now consider the positive side of the situation. There are two levels of computer use in any discipline: on the one hand, we find the expert, familiar with programming, hexadecimal, coping with diskette files, serial and parallel interfaces, and all the multitude of jargon-ridden horrors that beset the computer; on the other, we find the majority, the user who wants to apply the computer to his or her own discipline without being obliged to come to grips with every last complex detail of the machine. The latter expects to be able to use an off-the-peg package: SPSS for the social scientist, OCP for the literary scholar interested in analysing natural language, or one of the current authoring packages for someone wanting to get involved in CALL. (SPSS = Statistical Package for the Social Sciences; OCP = Oxford Concordance Program.)

So it is not necessary for every teacher to become an expert computer programmer in order to exploit the micro, in the same way that most of us happily drive a car without being excessively conscious of what goes on under the bonnet, since there are ready-made means in existence to help us to use the technology to a reasonable extent without our having to master the system in every last detail.

However, before going any further, there is one educational issue to be considered which has nothing to do with micros but a great deal to do with the attitudes of language teachers and, in particular, the theorists rather than the practitioners in language teaching. All disciplines are beset by constant swings of fashion – the historians oscillate between accounts of kings and queens on the one hand, and the social history of their meanest subjects on the other (the so-called new history), while the literary scholars swing from extrinsic to intrinsic, from structuralism to subjectivism – but it is in language teaching that these changing orthodoxies seem to be at their most extreme. The old order of grammar and compositional skills is swept aside to make way for communicative competence and role-playing, and instantly anyone using structured drills is regarded with the same kind of withering scorn as the scientist who persists in believing in the existence of phlogiston or the corpuscular theory of light.

The fact that communicative competence is currently all the rage should not mean that all other approaches to language learning are totally excluded. The various teaching strategies should not be mutually exclusive: teaching a language is a complex, messy business, in which different areas of language demand different tactics, even a modicum of drill and practice.

As far as language teaching is concerned, I belong to the school of bumbling eclecticism and hold the view that the various different lines of attack in language teaching should be mutually supportive. In my view, they need to be mixed in a manner which is appropriate both to the learners themselves and to their objectives in language learning, rather than to the theoretical stance adopted by the teacher, with no one particular method – especially in the case of drill and practice – isolated from the generality of the teaching strategy.

So you will find in these pages neither a doctrinaire approach to the teaching of language, nor an unquestioning eulogy of the computer as a panacea for the problems of language teaching; it *is* a limited tool, but, as I hope to demonstrate, within its limitations it has a very great potential for the teacher – and the learner – of languages.

2

The lessons of the past

Computers of one kind or another have been around for several decades, but the current flood of computing comics on the general market tends to give the reader the entirely erroneous impression that before the micro came upon the scene there was nothing. This is far from the truth, and it is important to lift the veil a little, find out what happened in the past, and see the lessons to be learned from what the early practitioners of literary and linguistic computing applications got up to; in other words, to discover whether we can at least help history to avoid repeating itself, and at best make advances on the basis of previous research and experience.

As you will have noticed, everything in computing tends to get boiled down to acronyms (the nicest I have encountered is COPE – Console Operator's Proficiency Examination), and the first use to which the linguists put the computer in its early days was that of MT (or, to spell it out in full, Mechanical Translation).

During the Second World War secret codes had become more and more complex, until the business of deciphering reached the point at which machines were required to assist in the laborious business of finding out what the enemy was saying (and sometimes, the cynic might say, what our own side might be trying to communicate). After hostilities ceased, academics in the USA, adopting a somewhat mechanistic view of language, argued that, if it is possible to translate from one code into another, then it should be relatively straightforward to translate from one natural language to another, for surely natural languages are nothing more than very complex codes.

It all began with a now famous – or infamous – memorandum written by Dr Warren Weaver in 1949 under the innocuous-sounding title 'Translation', in which he put forward the possibility of applying the computer in order to automate translation from one natural language to another.

In retrospect the naivety is almost painful, but so too is that of those in a more distant past to whom, given the current state of human knowledge, it seemed quite reasonable to postulate that the earth was flat or that it would be impossible for man to travel at more than twenty or so miles an hour without doing himself a permanent injury.

What had brought about the high level of interest in MT was the explosion – if explosion is the right word – in scientific knowledge after the end of the Second World War. Much of this took the form of periodical literature in a variety of languages, notably Russian and Chinese, and not many English and American scientists were sufficiently fluent in those tongues for them to be able to cope with Russian or oriental technical terminology.

The proponents of MT explored the possibility of applying the computer to the automatic translation of scientific documents and papers from these source languages into English. On a purely practical level, the task must have been daunting, since the valve computers of those days were not only horrendously unreliable and expensive in money and manpower, but also painfully slow by modern standards. In addition, they were designed as number-crunchers (jargon again – it means machines designed to perform huge calculations) rather than as devices for data processing (that is, the manipulation of information). The least of the difficulties that arose was the fact that the early machines had sparse provision for the special characters and dia-critics which the linguist requires, let alone the luxury of lower case characters. In addition, core storage (old technology computer memory) was at a premium, and MT involves much data-processing and a heavy use of computer memory.

On the theoretical plane, however, the early workers in the field fell foul of the fact that – *pace* East European linguists – the written language is not a complete code in itself which can be rendered automatically into another code, the target language, even via the intermediate stage of a metalanguage, a kind of halfway house between one language and another. All kinds of other factors interpose themselves: cultural references, puns, ambiguities, and the like. Even the apparent clinical purity of scientific language is not immune against the diversity and perversity of natural language. The human mind may be capable of deciphering the vagaries of natural language, but not the poor computer – yet. (I am using 'computer' here as a shorthand way of referring to the programs which drive the computer. The computer itself has no potential until programmed by human agency.)

What is the computer to make of translating a deliberate play on words like: 'He told the sexton, and the sexton tolled the bell?' The whole point of a pun is that it achieves the exact antithesis of the normal process of translating or interpreting a text: instead of resolving a complex pattern of possibilities into a single 'correct' rendition, the pun does exactly the reverse, leaving the MT program trying to jump down from the fence and run off in opposite directions simultaneously.

Favourites among the anecdotes in the mythology of MT relating to mistranslations caused by this kind of factor are the efforts of the computer to render into Russian idiomatic turns of phrase like 'The spirit is willing but the flesh is weak', which supposedly emerged as 'The vodka is OK but the meat is bad', or 'Out of sight, out of mind', which was rendered as 'Blind drunk'.

Professor Bar-Hillel of Jerusalem University took a lead in trying to bring sense into a somewhat Quixotic situation. He proposed (and, like all brilliant insights, it sounds self-evident once it has been said) that there were two possible approaches to MT: either you could have fully-mechanised, poor quality translations, or you could have high-quality translations using a judicious blend of computer and human editor. Thus was learned the first and, perhaps, most important lesson of computers and natural language: namely, that there is a considerable gulf between the two, and that this gulf must be both recognised (which is now fairly obvious) and exploited where appropriate (which is less obvious but has its applications). Or, to state the problem in a different way: the less ambitious the program – for example, a straightforward automatic dictionary – the more likely it is to be successful in collaboration with a human expert.

MT was rather like American man's first flight to the moon – the journey may not have been entirely necessary or even very productive in itself, but the spin-off was remarkably so. In learning that computers do not like giving 'perhaps' as an answer, linguists were forced into a less subjective definition of their terms of reference and into analysing language with greater precision. In addition, the lesson of the difference between the rigidity of the computer and the flexibility of the subjective individual had to be learned and, too, of the fact that language was not just another code.

So much for the meteoric rise and gradual decline of MT, which is now just beginning to re-emerge from obscurity thanks to another pressing demand for rapid multilingual translation generated by a new Tower of Babel, the Common Market. It is being explored in a multi-million project, Eurotra, the object of which is to seek computerised assistance in the crazy business of converting documentation into and from a whole mix of different languages. Like good Europeans (and like computer manufacturers too), the individual EEC states are quite happy to standardise on one language – as long as it is their own.

It was, in a sense, unfortunate that the original idea of MT came too much in advance of the ability of the technology then available to cope with it, but it now looks far more likely that MT of reasonable quality may be within our grasp; even now, in fact, there are commercially available packages which perform some of the routine tasks of translation, mainly on the lexical level.

The next significant historical application of the computer in the field of literary and linguistic computing was – surprisingly, perhaps – that of the concordance and similar investigations of literary texts.

The surprise is due to the innate conservatism of all but a handful of pre-structuralist literary scholars, many of whom, it seems, are still dubious about the merits of such dangerous innovations as those of Caxton; but most wondrous of all, it was the medievalists who took a lead in this field, notable among them R. A. Wisbey, founder of the Literary and Linguistic Computing Centre (LLCC) in the University of Cambridge, and now Professor of German at King's College London. Medievalists tend to be interested as much in the linguistic as in the literary aspects of their texts, and computer-ised analysis offered the prospect of detailed and far-ranging investigations which would be almost impossible by manual techniques. (It is, by the way, a curious fact that the majority of principal workers in the field of CALL and other computer applications in natural language are Germanists.)

A few enthusiasts came together and, building on the Newsletter edited by Joan M. Smith, then of UMRCC (University of Manchester Regional Computing Centre), founded the Association for Literary and Linguistic Com-puting (ALLC), which in 1983 celebrated ten years of existence, a membership approaching the thousand mark, and two publications, a Bulletin and a Journal. The first generally available concordance package, tastefully named COCOA (which stands for word COunt and COncordance generation on Atlas – the latter being the name of a computer), was devised by a team headed by Susan M. Hockey, the author of the standard history of literary and linguistic computing and leader of the team which put COCOA's successor together, the Oxford Concordance Program, to which reference was made earlier.

Before going any further, let us get some more jargon out of the way: a concordance differs from a word-index in that, whilst the latter is a straightforward list in alphabetical order of words in a given text, with page and line numbers alongside the words (it is sometimes called a KWOC index – Key-Word Out of Context), a full concordance gives, in addition to each alphabetised keyword, a context within which the keyword appears. In the case of poetry, the context is frequently the line of verse containing the keyword; in prose, the KWIC concordance predominates (Key-Word In Context), that is, the keyword is centralised on the page and a certain number of characters preceding and coming after the keyword are printed, usually more than enough for the word to be set in a meaningful context.

It was in the area of concordance generating that more of the historical lessons of computing and natural language began to emerge, the most important of which could be described as Murphy's Second Law of Computing, which states that: if ten scholars in ten ivory towers with ten computers each reinvented the wheel, that wheel would have ten different shapes, and few, if any, of them would be round.

Let us take as an example the generation of what, on the surface, appears to be a fairly straightforward concordance.

It sounds simplicity itself. The operation falls into three stages: (1) feed the text into the computer; (2) sort the words into alphabetical order; and (3) print them out with a context. As we shall see later, in relation to the student's response in tutorial-type CALL work, what appears at first sight to be child's play rapidly emerges as a complex minefield richly sown with anti-personnel devices for the unwary. Murphy's Third Law of Computing, then, states that simplicity is a phenomenon unknown in literary and linguistic computing (and this sad fact applies with equal force in all other areas of computing).

Let us consider each of these stages of generating a concordance in turn:

(1) Feed the text into the computer
In the case of a medieval epic, this is far from a simple matter: not only will our literary researcher have to decide what the text actually is (that is, which manuscript or edition to use for his database), but how to cope with ambiguities in the manuscripts, lacunae, and the like. Even with modern texts there are problems of variants, and once those have been resolved, there is the vexed question of pre-editing: how does one cope with, say, stage directions in a play, or with chapter or section titles in a novel? What about encoding exotic characters, the odd Greek word, and the like? Such problems are by no means as severe as they were in the pioneering days of concordances, when the first of the series of Cornell University concordances (which took as its subject the poetry of Matthew Arnold) had to face the uncomfortable fact that the IBM machine being used did not possess a single quotation mark or apostrophe on its print wheel, so 'she'll' and 'we'll' emerged as 'shell' and 'well'.

And that leads on to a much more vexed question: should the text be pre-edited to cope with homonyms (words with the same sound but different meanings, like 'spell', 'pore', 'date', 'rose', and many more), especially when there is no way of telling in advance which homonyms may be present? More of this problem in the next section.

(2) Sort the words into alphabetical order
Leaving aside the nightmarish problems of 'sorting' in languages like Chinese or Tibetan, the first question that arises is: what is a word? Take a simple example from German, an agglutinative language (one which builds up compounds): if, for example, you are interested in the use of the stem 'bau', how is that to be teased out of 'Zucker-rübenanbaugebiet' (sugar-beet growing area)? Equally problematical is the opposite situation in which the unit of meaning spreads over more than one word, for example, 'come', in such senses as 'a problem has come up', or 'We've just come by an antique wardrobe.' And that leads on to the

question of lemmatisation: should all the variations on 'come' ('came', 'coming', and the like) be grouped under the infinitive form? The wrong decision here can actually conceal information from the potential user: if, say, all forms of 'come up' are subsumed under one heading, a researcher interested in the use of 'up' in various verbal clusters will not be able to find what he or she is after.

(3) **Print the words in context**
The idea of printing each use of a word in its context is to give a clear notion of the way in which the word is being applied and of its precise significance.

The single-line context works in poetry for the most part, but can often lead to ambiguities (especially where homonyms occur), such as the second line of the famous Easter hymn:

> Without a city wall

Anyone unaware of the context beyond the words present might well conclude that 'without' is being applied in its familiar sense of 'lacking'.

Or again, if the meaning spreads over several lines problems can arise, as in this line from a sonnet dating back some four centuries by Sir William Alexander:

> And would of glorie challenge a reward.

What would challenge? (The answer in this case is 'haughtie thoughts', but without that information, there would be no way of finding out without tediously having to check manually through the original text.)

If this line of argumentation were followed through to its logical conclusion it would be necessary to print out at least the complete sentence in which the keyword occurs (or even, in certain circumstances, adjacent sentences), but this would present our literary scholar with a practical problem of (literally) staggering proportions. Imagine a text of 20,000 words, with an average sentence length of ten words: if each keyword were printed out together with a full sentence, the number of lines of output generated would cause our poor literary scholar to emerge from the local computing centre groaning under the weight of output, and facing the prospect of wading through far too much information in order to achieve the desired results.

Once again, the lesson to be learned is one of a reasonable compromise, a balance between man and machine, and one which should properly lead to a redefinition of the concept of 'publishing' a concordance: instead of – or as well as – a hard-copy final printout carried out within the terms of reference laid down by the editor and programmer, the original text should be available in machine-readable form, together with a package like OCP, which can interrogate the database selectively in response to requests from the researcher.

Earlier in this chapter, I referred to the fact that the differences between computer and natural language should not only be recognised, but also, where appropriate, exploited. This latter can be particularly apposite in the case of output from a computer-generated concordance, or concordance-type operation.

Computerised concordance output not only gives the researcher answers to specific questions posed, such as, for example, how and when Shakespeare employs imagery relating to extra-terrestrial objects (sun, stars, moon, comets, and the like); it can also produce unexpected information because of the different way in which the computer 'perceives' a text (or indeed data of any kind). This concept is a crucial one for practitioners of CALL, and it is therefore necessary for us to explore it in a little detail.

Let me take a parallel from audio tape recording: if you make a sound recording of, say, an interview in a private house, you will 'hear' the words of the interviewer and interviewee while you make the recording, because you are concentrating on them and excluding 'extraneous' sounds from your mind; when, however, you play back your precious recording you may well find it ruined by the loud ticking of a clock, the crackling of the fire, or the snoring of the dog.

This kind of selectivity of perception, which we practise every moment of our waking lives, is not granted to machines; equally, in a literary text, an author will deliberately highlight certain words and phrases, and allow others to fade into the background. The computer, however, takes each unit of the text as a chunk of data with no more or less significance than the next.

This means that the output from a concordance can generate quite surprising insights. Here is one specific example from my own work with computers. The German essayist and poet Fritz Usinger, who died in 1983, wrote a collection of poems entitled *Canopus*, which I fed into the computer and analysed for an article to be included in his eighty-fifth birthday *Festschrift*. After producing a concordance, word frequency count, and the like, I 'doodled' on the computer terminal, generating listings of various combinations of characters ('end', for example), and just tried listing all the occurrences of commas in the text in a KWIC listing.

To my great surprise, the results were far from trivial. Usinger's view of the cosmos is such that, without going into technicalities, it caused him to think in terms of units of three, of a tripartite division, and the listing of commas revealed what I would never have noticed had I read *Canopus* again and again; namely, that the units of three also found their way into the sentence structure of the poetry, not often, but always in important places; and the computer listing made this immediately obvious.

However, the concordance and its derivatives far from exhaust the possibilities of quantitative analysis of literary and non-literary texts. There are, one might say, far more interesting things that you can do with a book than actually read it, as computer applications in language and literature demonstrate, and I now turn briefly to survey a representative selection of other such applications in order to explore further the lessons of the past.

A particularly unkind reviewer once wrote about a less than brilliant Shakespearian performance that the issue of authorship could now at last be resolved by digging up Marlowe, Shakespeare and other aspirants and ascertaining which of them had turned over in his grave. With the advent of the computer, however, it seemed that a sounder and more scientific approach than the spade might now be available to the researcher anxious to explore such issues as disputed authorship (who wrote what), given the machine's insatiable appetite for handling vast quantities of data without getting bored or making mistakes.

Unfortunately, the golden maxim of computing – 'garbage in, garbage out' – holds good in this sphere as in any other. There are two broad approaches that can be adopted to disputed authorship: the first involves feeding the raw text into the machine and using it as a fairly blunt instrument for determining average word or sentence length. Vocabulary size and distribution can also be examined in this manner.

The second approach involves either heavy pre-editing of the text or running it through one of the syntactical analysis programs available, in order to explore the variations in stylistic patterns.

In any event, as the innocent-looking words 'average', 'distribution', and 'patterns' suggest, it is more than likely that the researcher will need to wander into the quagmire of statistics. Although techniques have been devised for the statistical analysis of natural language, considerable difficulties need to be overcome in the application of statistics in this area. The lesson to be learned here is that, in the relations between computer and natural language, the researcher has to acquire whole new areas of skill before sensible progress can be made. This will certainly emerge as the case with CALL: it is not simply a matter of 'knowing' about your own discipline (literary analysis, linguistics, or whatever), and just grafting on to that enough knowledge of computing to get by: those two skills are just the raw materials, as it were, on the basis of which new skills have to be acquired in order to produce sensible results and genuine progress.

In statistics, frequency of occurrence of an item within a known population is a significant feature. But in language, two particular problems arise. First: what is the population? If so many drivers are arrested for drunken driving in any given year, it is easy to express that figure as a percentage, since the total overall number of drivers is known (although, of course, some cover only a short distance in a given year, whilst others drive tens of thousands of miles), but there is no way of knowing the total 'population' (vocabulary) of a writer. Even if all his works are fed into the computer and the number of different words counted up, that does not prove that those are all the words the writer 'knows'. Secondly, frequency of occurrence is not always significant: variations in the number of drivers arrested for drunkenness can be attributed to the advent of various festive seasons, but sometimes a word or phrase used only once in a key position has a vital role to play in an individual text, and even the absence of a word or phrase can be of great significance when its presence might be expected.

Once again, it is a sensitive and intelligent cooperation between computer and expert interpreter which can produce the best results. In the context of frequency, where words occur can be of great significance, and 'positional stylometry', as it is called, can serve as a very significant contributor to an understanding of a stylistic analysis of a particular text.

In this area, the differences between computer and natural language can further be exploited by concentrating on this relationship between 'quantity' and 'quality' in the analysis and evaluation of a literary text (or, indeed, of any other kind of text). This can perhaps best be illustrated by an interactive technique I developed for an undergraduate Honours Special

Subject course on computational stylistics in the University of Hull. (Courses of this nature were then, and still are, something of a rarity.)

The practical element of the course included students seated at a computer terminal being invited to interrogate a literary text using a fairly simple-minded interactive program. This first asks which string (computer jargon for unbroken sequence) of characters, which can include spaces and punctuation marks, the user wishes to search for in the text that has been selected. Once the search is completed, the program puts up on the screen the number of occurrences, if any, of the string which it has found in the text, and invites the user to request a full listing of occurrences, either on the screen or in hard copy, or both.

The output was in the form of page and line number, followed by a KWIC-type listing of the occurrences. Then the user was invited to search for another string. By this means it proved possible to build up a quantitative profile of a given text on the basis of an initial request followed by further requests for searches, building all the while on the knowledge gained. Perhaps the technique will make a lot more sense if an illustration is provided.

The text used to demonstrate the technique to students was a nineteenth-century German short story by Heinrich von Kleist, entitled 'Das Bettelweib von Locarno' (The Beggar Woman of Locarno.) Kleist's style is distinctive and unusual in that he characteristically uses long, complex sentences, and at certain points in the narrative employs favourite key phrases. In a typical session at the keyboard, the student would first be invited to request a search for full stops in the text. This yielded a figure of 20 occurrences, and the student was asked to build up a hypothesis on sentence structure in the text, given the great length of the sentences which the listing revealed.

The student might assume that the connectives 'und' ('and') and 'aber' ('but') might play an important part in the text, and would then ask for listings of those strings. The search for 'und', however, yields two unexpected results: the first is that there are very few occurrences of 'und' linking clauses, and the second is that where the word occurs it is most frequently linking two descriptors. Hence the student is forced to adopt a different hypothesis in relation to sentence structure (namely, that there must be a great deal of sub-ordination, relative clauses and the like), and subsequently investigates further the chance revelation of Kleist's predilec-tion for pairing descriptors.

Once a detailed investigation of the text based on this kind of procedure has been completed and a stylistic profile has been built up on the basis of quantitative information, the student is then invited to consider the relationship between quantity and quality; that is, to what extent questions of how often, how infrequently, and where, can profitably lead on to an aesthetic evaluation of the text. The answer is a very positive one, not least because the technique forces the student to concentrate on the text without preconceptions and to develop strategies, on or off the computer, for the critical investigation of natural language texts.

The quantitative investigations of Swift by L. T. Milic present further insights into the possibilities of this kind of approach, which are important also in the area of attribution studies (who wrote what). Milic postulates two constituents in a writer's style, which he dubs conscious and unconscious style. Conscious style is context-bound: if an author is writing about bee-keeping there will be much stinging and buzzing, and references to hives, drones, royal jelly and the like. Unconscious style is, to borrow an awful term from town planning, a kind of infrastructure to support and sustain any context. A writer may, for example, tend to develop an argument in a particular manner, using phrases like 'on the one hand', 'it may be seen that', or he may hedge his statements, as I have done a couple of times in this chapter, with conditional terms like 'may', 'might', and 'perhaps'. Such formulae, it is argued, will be present whatever the context. In Kleist, for example, the phrase 'dergestalt, dass' ('in such a way that') occurs at the culminating point of the story about the beggar woman, but also elsewhere in his work in similar situations.

Related to this approach is the application of DBM (database management) techniques to the investigation of literary texts, either by adapting existing concordance programs or by employing off-the-shelf packages from manufacturers or software houses. One recent study has adopted this approach in the analysis of the style of *Paradise Lost*, demonstrating, for example, the way in which the vocabulary of individual characters in the poem varies according to who else is present.

There are many other such techniques, some simple, some sophisticated, some successful, others less so, for the investigation and evaluation of natural language texts: collocational studies seeking to arrive, if possible, at a definitive version of a text pose all manner of serious challenges to the programmer; graph theory has been adapted to the textual analysis of manuscripts in an attempt to establish which order the manuscripts were written in; and even specialist scientific techniques like spectral analysis have been brought into play in phonological studies of natural language text. And the body of research work is growing in breadth and quantity almost daily.

In conclusion, then, the lessons to be learned from the applications of the computer, past and present, to language and literature can be summarised in these terms:

(1) To state the obvious, which to some researchers is unfortunately not so obvious, there are considerable differences between the computer and natural language. The former is concerned entirely with unambiguous, quantifiable information, whereas the latter is an enormously complex expression of a whole culture at a given point in time. As a result, there are many functions which a computer cannot readily perform – yet. The technology

is developing at such a rapid pace that even tasks which now appear far beyond the capability of the machine may not be so in 20 or 30 years' time. As a result of these limitations, it is wise counsel to concentrate on those areas in which the computer can perform efficiently and yield meaningful results, rather than seek to force it into unsuitable roles. It is, for example, quite a trivial programming matter to ask the computer to yield up the occurrences of specified strings, but not, say, of adjectives in a text, unless there is a vast dictionary look-up table of adjectives stored in the machine – and even then there would be problems with homonyms like 'green', 'tender', and many more. Hence the computer is better at detecting specific instances within a text than broad general features of that text.

(2) Once these differences have been recognised, they can, of course, be exploited. The computer's 'perception' of a text is different from that of the human reader, since it works entirely in terms of quantities.

(3) Thus it is wrong to expect the computer to perform unaided a vastly complex task like MT; a productive collaboration between man and machine yields the best results. The computer cannot – yet – operate in the same way as the human brain, taking imaginative leaps and cutting through a tangled web of argument to arrive at new insights.

(4) On a more jaundiced note, there is no such thing as a 'simple' computer program. Tasks which we regard as simple can be very complex for the computer, and, in the last analysis, unprogrammable given the current state of knowledge and technology.

(5) It should not be thought that the application of the computer to natural language is just a matter of learning how to program (which in itself is no mean feat); techniques and skills for employing the computer in this role also have to be mastered.

(6) Given the limitations, the problems, the skills to be

acquired, it appears to be a daunting and restricted tool, but this is far from being the case. Once the computer has been mastered, it is quite astonishing how the ingenuity of researchers, particularly, as we shall see, in CALL, have exploited the machine in all kinds of different ways.

Having considered the background to CALL, we now take a look at the hardware which supports CALL, and then turn to the development and use of CALL itself.

3

The micro comes upon the scene: the hardware

Up until now, whenever I have used the word 'computer', I have been employing the term as a shorthand way of saying 'mainframe (electronic digital) computer'. Computers fall into three broad categories, each of which has its own buzz-word.

Mainframe computers are usually large systems, filling rooms with cabinets housing the main store, and other devices such as the ALU (Arithmetic and Logic Unit), multiplexers, communications processors and the like, disk and magnetic tape drives, paper tape readers and punches, card readers and punches, high-speed line printers, graph plotters, and much more besides. The environment is air-conditioned (to maintain a stable temperature and humidity and to minimise dust particles), and the whole system requires a considerable staff to operate, maintain, and program it.

The *minicomputer* is a boiled down version of the mainframe and is much more compact, requires less staff and a less rigidly controlled environment, but is typically much more powerful in terms of size and speed than an older mainframe costing many times more.

The *microcomputer* requires only a desk-top and access to the normal mains supply, or – with the advent of the truly portable micro – a rechargeable battery and an executive's knee to sit on.

Over the years, the price of computing has plummeted and reliability has increased beyond all recognition. As a result, the micro, either as a dedicated microprocessor (one that performs only a limited, pre-programmed set of operations, like a supermarket checkout cash register or an automated teller outside a bank) or as a general purpose computer, is spreading into every area of our lives. Whereas a couple of years ago I would have been typing the manuscript of this book on a golfball typewriter, I am now using a micro as a word processor to prepare it. The output on floppy disk can be sent directly to a computerised phototypesetter.

Most importantly, the micro has freed computing facilities from the clutches of the experts. The majority of micros are sold over the counter or by mail order to non-expert users, and this has forced upon the developers of packages for the business and hobbyist user a new approach to computer applications. No longer is the user obliged to learn one or more complex computer language in order to make the machine function; 'turn-key' packages (that is, packages which require little more than a knowledge of how to switch the machine on) enable naive users to employ the micro as a word processor, stock controller, accountant, or in a host of other roles.

One point which should be made here in passing about the first micros, and one to which far too little attention has been paid, is the unlovely appearance of most of the early micros. They had all the aesthetic charm (for those with long memories) of a bakelite wireless set, and it is only now that the manufacturers are really turning their attention to the physical appearance of their equipment that the products are presenting themselves as professionally constructed machines for the general market rather than string and sealing wax kits for the devoted amateur. In the past, there has been far too little concern with the design of the products; and, given the scepticism of the language teacher, a less than attractive keyboard housing, sprayed in a delicate shade of black and trailing coaxial cable to a tank-like monitor, is hardly likely to convert him or her to microcomputing overnight.

This rapid technological change has brought with it one

very difficult challenge for the teacher which has been given the delightful title of the 'upwards embarrassment factor'. In other words, youngsters of eight or nine are neither intimidated nor bemused by the micro but learn to operate it with amazing rapidity, whereas their teacher, brought up in an age when biros were frowned upon and the only mechanical guides to computation were the slide rule and books of tables, is confronted with a whole new area of knowledge which is advancing at a frightening rate.

Perhaps we should briefly consider what is meant by the term 'micro', which I have been employing with such gay abandon. I have been using the word as a convenient abbreviation for 'microcomputer', which consists of a 'microprocessor' linked typically with a keyboard, a screen, and some kind of external storage medium. The microprocessor consists of the famous silicon (not silicone!) chip – which is most likely a LSI chip (meaning Large Scale Integration, that is, with a large number of functions on one chip) – containing the memory, other chips holding disk controllers, character sets, and other software, and various other specialised circuits. In order to examine the potential of the micro in language teaching, we must be clear as to the nature of most of these features. The reader who is thoroughly conversant with the micro can skip what follows. This is intended only as a general introduction from the viewpoint of the language teacher, not as a comprehensive guide to the current state of the market.

Every general-purpose micro I have seen has a QWERTY (that is, standard typewriter) keyboard of some kind or other, from the touch-sensitive variety at the lower end of the market to rugged keyboards with moving keys at the other. In addition to the normal alphanumeric characters (that is, A – Z, a – z, and 0 – 9), punctuation, and various other keys (brackets, dollar signs, etc.), many of which are in infuriatingly different locations on different machines, the computer keyboard has additional keys which mark it off from the standard typewriter. They fall into three categories:

(1) the five keys which are usually marked with arrows, and normally allow you to move the cursor in the directions of the four points of the compass, and to the 'home' position at the top lefthand corner of the screen. The cursor is a 'blip' or blob which either blinks or is steady (according to a switch setting on the machine), the purpose of which is to inform you 'where you are now' on the screen: where, in other words, the next character will come when you type it. The computer can be programmed to move the cursor around the screen in a variety of ways, and this facility has considerable potential for the languages user.

(2) The 'control' key, usually marked 'CTRL', which, when depressed in conjunction with other keys, generates special functions. For example, 'CTRL' plus I has an effect similar to that of the tabulator on a conventional typewriter, and 'CTRL' plus C in some environments loads or reloads the operating system (this is what the jargon quaintly calls a cold or warm boot).

(3) Often there are special fixed or programmable function keys, which can be used as shorthand for full commands.

Foreign language accents and exotic character sets, like Cyrillic or Greek, which in the early days presented considerable problems to the literary or linguistic user, are becoming increasingly simple to represent on the screen using a variety of techniques.

The housing for the keyboard frequently contains the microprocessor and other chips, together with a number of sockets for linking it to other elements of the computer.

One element which is almost invariably connected to the keyboard is a CRT terminal (Cathode Ray Tube), in plain English a TV screen; this can be either a standard black and white or colour receiver, or – much more desirably – a specialised high definition monitor which reduces eyestrain, has much greater definition, and can improve the graphics capability, especially in colour, beyond all recognition.

Colour monitors are often referred to as RGB monitors, that is, they take in the red, green and blue signals separately, with a resultant increase in sharpness of definition.

What you type at the terminal will appear ('be echoed', to use the jargon) on the CRT. Apart from normal white on a black ground, the micro can generate characters in inverse video (black on white), underlined, in blink mode (flashing on and off, or from one colour to another), or in low intensity for a variety of different effects.

Now we turn to the external storage media. If you type a program or data into the computer and then switch it off, you will typically 'lose' all that information from what the jargon calls the 'volatile memory' of the machine, and it would be a somewhat crazy situation if every program had to be typed in anew every time the computer is switched on. Some of the computer's memory is non-volatile, and this is usually in the form of ROM (read-only memory), which might contain the instructions which run the operating system, a word-processing package, a computer game, or a programming language like BASIC; for the most part, however, some means or other of storing information in a more or less permanent manner is required.

The cheapest, least reliable, and slowest such medium is the standard cassette tape recorder. Programs and data can be copied to and from cassette, but reliability can pose a problem. If you are making an ordinary audio recording (using the normal analogue approach), a fault in the tape just causes a temporary but irritating loss of sound called 'drop-out'; if, however, you are recording digital computer information, then the problem is fatal, since programs and data are held as 'blips', or individual bits of information, each one of which is both significant and crucial to an understanding by the computer of what is stored. Various ways round this problem have been devised, but these only make the least attractive aspect of cassette recording even worse, namely, the slow speed of reading from the cassette and writing to it. For this reason alone, cassettes as storage media are in my view out of the question for CALL applications, except in very limited special circumstances.

The other common, but much more expensive, external storage medium is the floppy disk (*sic*) drive. Once the drive has been purchased, however, the disks themselves are inexpensive and highly reliable. They consist of flat discs of material like magnetic tape in a protective sleeve. Access time (the amount of time required to locate information for reading and writing) can be counted in parts of a second rather than, with the cassette, in seconds - or even minutes. One disadvantage is that of lack of standardisation from one machine to another: disks can, for example, be either single or double density ('density' refers to the amount of information that can be packed on to a disk), single or double sided (information can be stored in the latter case on both sides of the disk), floppy or mini-floppy (8 inches or 5¼ inches), and the variations do not end there by any means.

This is not the place for a detailed consumers' association report on the available hardware, not least since expertise in this area is readily available to many educationalists from their purchasing officers or their equivalent, but the following crucial points must be borne in mind:

(1) A machine at the bottom end of the market is not likely to be rugged enough for educational use, and it may soon prove the case with such equipment that its limitations are too severe for any but the least demanding tasks. A very cheap machine is less likely to be expandable or – to use the jargon – 'futureproof', that is, compatible with new developments in hardware and software. It is also less likely to have all the connectors to the outside world, to have high definition monitors or serial ports to communicate with other equipment.

(2) If courseware from outside sources is required, or courseware that you generate is also destined for external use, the problem of portability of programs and data arises. Remember particularly that there are as many

(in fact, probably more!) different BASICs as there are microcomputers, each 'dialect' having its own variations, restrictions, and idiosyncracies.

(3) In my view, the minimum configuration for a micro destined for CALL use is 16K RAM storage (in non-technical terms enough memory for the user to write to and read from) at the very least, a reasonable-quality screen (preferably a monitor, and nowadays a colour one), access to disk storage, and at least a dot matrix printer (a printer which produces text by means of a pattern of little dots on the paper, and which is cheaper than a daisywheel printer).

This may seem a counsel of perfection in hard financial times, or where a purchasing authority decides to 'standardise' on one particular machine (often for central bulk purchasing convenience rather than in recognition of the varying needs of different establishments and disciplines). However, the kind of performance which you get from a micro is – as is the case with other consumer durables – more or less directly proportional to the purchase price, and there is little point in acquiring the computing equivalent of a moped and expecting it to cope with motorway conditions.

Perhaps the best advice is the old adage of *caveat emptor*, coupled with the need to discuss with others who have already acquired computing hardware before purchasing equipment in haste, the acquisition of which you will have much leisure to repent. It is important to gain access to the decision makers if the voice of the language teacher is to be heard when computing equipment is purchased so that, for example, a computer with programmable character sets is purchased, and printers with similar facilities, rather than a machine which suits the purposes of one section only; computers are, after all, supposed to be for use across the curriculum.

4

A CALL case history I: design and implementation

I now turn to the way in which the computer has been applied to CALL, from off-the-peg material requiring no programming knowledge at all, via authoring packages which permit you to write courseware with little or no knowledge of programming, to what the expert 'DIY' programmers have been up to in the field. But it is first necessary to consider in some depth the theoretical and practical issues surrounding CALL.

Perhaps the best way to examine these issues is to describe a case history in some detail, and to try and draw a number of generally valid conclusions from past blunders. So, to avoid self and publisher being dragged into libel suits, let me describe my own first attempts at CALL in the German Department in the University of Hull some eight years ago.

At that time I was using a mainframe computer, of course, but the lessons to be learned are broadly the same as those that can be drawn from designing a package on a micro. CALL techniques tend not to be specific to one kind of computer nor to any particular type of package; what is, however, essential, is that the painful process of learning by mistakes is gone through (preferably not too often, and by someone else) before the necessary expertise is acquired.

The package came into being in the first place not out of any macho desire to sire a CALL package for the sake of it, but in answer to a specific need. First, like all good packages, it had to be given a name. With devastating originality, I decided to christen it EXERCISE.

For the first time, a beginners' course in German had been initiated in Hull, and it rapidly became clear that the number of contact hours available were far from adequate for giving the students time for drill and practice. However unappetising it may seem, there is no escaping the awkward fact that language learning is unique among disciplines in that it requires the learner somehow or other to bridge the gap between knowing as an intellectual fact that 'das Haus' is the German for 'the house' and being able to recall it instantly and in its correct form. However this gap between passive and active knowledge is overcome, overcome it must be.

In the intensive conditions of the course, the students actually asked for question and answer exercises. (I hasten to add, for those of a nervous disposition, that this was all within the wider context of a course which actually concentrated on communicative skills.)

I decided to try and devise a computer package which would enable the learner to use a terminal as an ersatz teacher for the specific purpose of drill and practice. (A terminal is a work station connected to a computer, and usually consists of a keyboard linked either to a teleprinter or a TV monitor.)

A word of explanation: a package is a suite of programs which perform all aspects of a particular task. Hence the EXERCISE package consisted not just of a program which tested the learner, but also a program to enable the non-expert teacher to input and edit course material, and another utility to list courseware and monitor output (of which more in a moment).

A number of lessons were rapidly learned, not so much by the students as by myself as test designer.

The first relates to what might be termed the 'signal to noise' ratio in educational technology. In theory, the educational element should dominate, whilst in the background the technology purrs unobtrusively and efficiently. Murphy's Fourth Law of Computing, however, states that there is an inverse relationship between the level of technology involved and the chances of its working faultlessly on the day. Not much harm is done if a piece of chalk breaks in two, nor a great deal more if a projector bulb pops or a tape winds itself round the capstan, but when close on a million pounds' worth of computer decides to throw a tantrum the results from an educational point of view can be little short of disastrous.

When, for example, a student sitting at a terminal keys in a response, he or she may have to sit waiting for the machine to talk back. The wait time could be caused either by the fact that the student has failed to hit the appropriate button to tell the machine that it is the computer's turn to contribute something; or that the machine is busy dealing with other people's programs (the variations in response time – that is, the time it takes the computer to respond – were infuriatingly unpredictable); or that the machine has broken down, and that the part of the machine which sends to the terminal an error message to that effect has itself broken down (a not uncommon occurrence).

In the micro environment, most but not all of these failings are likely to occur, although the level of control which the programmer has with a micro means that they can be much more readily overcome. If, for example, the learner fails to hit the 'return' key on a micro, it is possible to program the machine to wait for a specified number of seconds, and if no response from the keyboard is forthcoming, a gentle reminder can be flashed on to the screen.

It is not, however, just the level of technology that presents problems: the sheer complexity of learning to communicate with a mainframe computer is itself quite daunting. The man–machine interface (jargon for the means of communicating between man and machine) on the Hull ICL1904S is designed to frighten the life out of the first-time user. In addition, the only terminals available were noisy teleprinters with upper case letters only. Given all these problems and more besides, I decided that, if a CALL package could be persuaded to work in this hostile environment, it would work anywhere.

It required a great deal of ingenuity to overcome the man–machine interface problems on the ICL1904S, and, in fact, these were never entirely overcome. To enable a user to communicate with the computer for the first time required a ten-minute video recording I had made together with an eight-page booklet covering all aspects of the machine and the package. Still, the students overcame these problems with remarkable rapidity, and were soon sitting at the terminal swearing at the computer like old hands. This gave me good reason to believe that, in happier circumstances, students would adapt with even greater ease to the computer. Educationalists tend as a breed to underestimate the learner's ability to overcome technical problems, and this is as true of computing as it is of other disciplines.

In the micro environment, however, these can be resolved by devising a 'turnkey system' in which all the specialised knowledge the user requires is how to switch the micro on (i.e. turn the key) and insert a diskette into the drive. The program then takes over, guiding him if he makes mistakes, and should be sufficiently robust (i.e. crashproof, or – even more of a challenge – studentproof) to cope even with deliberate abuse of the terminal. By 'abuse' I do not mean verbal but rather physical maltreatment of the keyboard, deliberately hitting the wrong keys in an attempt to cause the package to crash. (In the micro environment, this problem can be overcome by programming the keys on the keyboard – especially the 'break' and 'escape' keys – in such a way that, to use the technical term, they are 'disabled', and do not perform their normal functions of halting the program or resetting the whole system.)

The EXERCISE package, once loaded by the student, offers assistance if the user is at a loss as to how to proceed. For example, if the name of an exercise is mistyped, three options are offered:

(1) the student can make another attempt at typing the name;

(2) he or she can opt for a list of exercises and/or subject areas available;

(3) he or she can abandon the session.

The second lesson to be learned by myself as test designer was that it is crucial to achieve a thoroughly sound basic design. At this point, two key decisions have to be taken by the designer: the first concerns the relationship between the data and the program, the second – which can only be taken on the basis of the first decision – concerns the design concept of the actual package.

There are two general approaches to the design of a package in this field (as indeed, in many others): the programmer can opt either for a 'dedicated' program, or a 'context-free' program (the latter is similar in approach to the notion of a 'template' program, which you may well come across in CALL literature). The accompanying diagram gives a rough idea of the difference between the two. In a dedicated

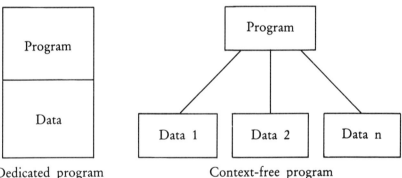

Dedicated program   Context-free program

program, the data and the program are inextricably bonded to one another: such a program designed, say, to test all the possible combinations of all the German strong verbs will do that, and nothing more. On the positive side, it is possible to make the program perform that task with great subtlety, taking into account every possible nuance, all the oddities and irregularities, and coping also with different kinds of learner who require varying degrees of speed and difficulty.

However, the penalty for this kind of approach is a severe one indeed: much of the programming effort is absorbed into this one-off program (some routines may, of course, be generalisable – that is, usable in other similar programs), and the man-hours required for the creation of such a program may well be out of all proportion to the limited benefit to the learner, who, if the program is successful, will soon be clamouring for similar programs on adjectival endings, word order, and so on. In addition, it is clear that a considerable amount of input in terms of both time and effort is demanded for each such project on the part both of the programmer and of the linguist. Good and frequent communication is demanded between both, and both may feel constrained by limitations imposed by the other.

The alternative approach is a 'context-free', or 'generalised' program. Let us take a very simple-minded example to illustrate the difference. If we wrote a little program which asked the learner to give us the plural of 'cat', and incorporated into the program the correct answer, 'cats', we should have a pretty limited dedicated program. If, however, we designed a program which would put any noun from a stored list on to the screen, assuming it is a regular noun with 's' as plural, then the program would have considerably more value, but a somewhat severe limitation. Modifications to the data, which would pair singulars and plurals, would enable us to cope, not only with 'batch – batches' and 'wife – wives' but also with wildly irregular forms like 'mouse – mice'. In other words, detaching the data from the program (although it may impose limitations on flexibility) considerably increases the potential for using one program on a vast range of data.

Our program can now cope with any pair of items of quantifiable information, and match it with the learner's response; so it need not simply take the form of singular plus plural, it could be pronoun for noun, ordinal for cardinal (or even the country of which X is the capital city, the year King Y died in, or a series of true or false responses).

So a generalisable program will be able to operate on a

considerable range of data, but the penalty here may be that of reduced flexibility. For example, to return to the German strong verbs, the dedicated program would readily be able to cope with the problems thrown up by 'müssen – muss', and give the learner special tuition on the present tense difficulties of the preterite present verbs, but this may well present problems for the context-free program, unless it is particularly well designed. And it is to this key problem that I now turn.

There are two basic approaches to programming a problem and in the charming jargon of computer folk, these are described as 'top down' and 'bottom up'. The former implies working from the general to the particular, the latter the reverse. In CALL design 'bottom up' is, in my view, the only viable approach, since we are primarily concerned with the nature of the interaction between learner and computer. All else should be built around this central core. Once a sound fundamental concept has been perfected, it is quite amazing how much can be built up around a central core, even one as seemingly trivial as that for the EXERCISE package. In abstract terms the basic concept of the package can be described thus:

(COMMENT +) QUESTION + ANSWER(S) (+ COMMENT)

The bracketed items are optional. If the above representation is less than helpful, what it means is that the package was built round the core of a question plus answer(s), with comments randomly interspersed anywhere except between question and answer.

Here is a simple example which, it must be stressed, is not of any great educational merit, but which is designed to demonstrate the features – and weaknesses – of the package:

Comment: This is Exercise No. 99
            In this exercise please write in full the
            German for the following numbers.

Question: 33
Answer: dreiunddreissig
Comment: Do remember that 'dreissig' is the odd man
            out among the numbers 20 – 90. The others
            are regular but there's a slight catch in the
            next one. . .
Question: 66
Answer: sechsundsechzig
. . . etc.

When the learner loads this imaginary Exercise No. 99, the teleprinter types the introductory comment, followed by the question, and invites the learner to respond. It all seems simplicity itself. Or is it?

Murphy's Fifth Law of Computing restates the Iceberg Principle: namely that, for every single visible effect in computing, (a) a great deal of work has been going on below the surface; and (b) a titanic design effort has gone into getting it right. In other words, what the learner sees and does constitutes only a tiny portion of the total package. I have already referred to routines to help if he or she mistypes the name of an exercise (and the reason that Exercise No. 99 starts by identifying itself is in case the learner had meant to type 98 but had missed – there is a built-in panic button to allow escape from an exercise at any point). But it was also necessary to write a set of routines to enable teachers who know little or nothing about computing to type in and edit their own exercises, and a number of other utilities had to be devised.

However, to return specifically to the exercise about numbers and its apparent simplicity: the computer sits waiting for the learner to respond to the first question. The learner goes into a trance-like state of concentration, takes a deep breath – and starts to key in an answer. The trouble is that he or she might type, equally correctly, any one of the following – assuming an upper and lower case keyboard (the strange symbol ▽ means space):

dreiunddreissig
∇ ∇ Dreiunddreissig
DREIUNDDREISSIG.
Is it dreiunddreissig?

The computer takes every incoming character literally, so it has to be trained in this instance to ignore superfluous spaces and punctuation, and to consider upper and lower case letters of the alphabet as direct equivalents.

One of the severest criticisms directed against the drill and practice supporters is that they can tend to place accuracy on a pedestal and largely ignore fluency and communication. The story of the school in the midst of the African bush puts the case at its most extreme. A class is learning English. Scene one: the best child in the class looks out of the window, raises his hand, and starts the following sentence: 'Please teacher, sir, I was looking out of the window just now, and I could see that a large lion was making his way . . .' By the time the star pupil has got this far, the whole class has been eaten. Scene two: the worst child in the class looks out of the window, shouts 'Big cat him come', and they all hear, understand and are saved.

The trouble is that the two camps tend to see no good at all in the other side; if, however, drill and practice are tempered by a less than total desire for accuracy, and placed in an appropriate wider teaching context, they have a great deal to offer – the only question in relation to CALL is, how can this be achieved without making the programming hopelessly complex or the writing of courseware infinitely tedious?

This is not an easy area from a programming point of view, although, at first sight, the notion of accepting – either in the sense of recognising or marking as correct – a 'nearly right' answer seems very attractive and not too difficult to implement, until, that is, one begins to consider the problems arising from an attempt to design a generalised algorithm (procedure which breaks a problem down into a series of logical steps).

The easiest situation to deal with is one in which the

learner mistypes upper for lower case, and vice versa, since it is simplicity itself to program the computer to regard upper and lower case as identical, and, in addition, to build in a routine which can distinguish between upper and lower case when the courseware designer requires it. An example is an exercise testing the learner's ability to remember that nouns in German tend to begin with an upper case letter, when 'Haus' would be accepted, but not 'haus'.

It is also easy to cause irrelevant spaces and punctuation to be ignored on the same basis; but, as will readily be seen, these are really issues on the periphery of the main problem, that of somehow recognising that the learner has got the essence of the answer correct, perhaps for example by typing 'dreiundreisig'. The programming problem is: how can a generalisable routine be written which can cope with this kind of situation?

There are two approaches which can be adopted: in the first, the 'responsibility' is taken by the program, in the second, by the courseware designer.

The first approach would be to write a generally applicable algorithm which would somehow discount certain classes of error, that is, to accept a 'nearly right' response. This approach is, however, fraught with difficulty. What if the routine accepted transposed letters? This would not be so serious with 'dreiunddriessig', perhaps, but 'furchtbar' (frightful) and 'fruchtbar' (fruitful) could be a fatal error, as could 'cieling' in a test of the 'i before e' rule in English.

Accepting one character less or more than the right answer might equally seem attractive, but if the learner is trying to master English, for example, 'he come' is not an acceptable 'near miss' for 'he comes'.

The central issue here is that of the badly designed CALL program which states that a response is either right or wrong, but gives no help at all in the latter case.

One approach is to give the courseware designer the option of using 'wild cards', as they are called, that is, of using dummy characters: the normal convention is that ? is employed to replace any one character, whilst * is set aside to replace any number of characters, including no character at all.

There are other halfway houses between right and wrong which can be adopted on a generalised basis. The computer can be programmed to indicate where a learner has started to go wrong in the answer, for example, by mistyping 'dreiunddreissig' by omitting the double d, and he or she can then be invited to try again.

Equally, the 'shape' of the answer can be given in the form of crosses, as in this case: 'The cat sat on the xxx', again guiding the learner in the direction of the correct response

In all this, it must of course be borne in mind that it is the responsibility of the designer of the program and of the courseware to ensure that these techniques are properly applied. If they are not, it is not the fault of the computer.

Having said all that, perhaps the key issue lies outside the province of CALL altogether: the real problem is that what is an 'acceptable' example in one set of circumstances ('Big cat him come') may be far from acceptable with the same or a different learner in different circumstances. By this I mean that 'drieunddriessig' may well be acceptable if the emphasis is placed on the pattern of the German numerals system, in which 'three and thirty' is the pattern, but would be a far from acceptable response when the differences between the pronunciation of 'ie' and 'ei' in English and German are being tested. (For those unfamiliar with the problem, it can best be summarised by the neat little mnemonic about pronunciation in German: 'Never say die.')

But what if the learner keys in the wrong response altogether? An important design decision, based (it must be confessed) in the first instance on pure guesswork, was that of how many attempts the learner should be permitted at each question. Two attempts seemed a reasonable compromise, both in order to give the learner an opportunity to think again but – it is hoped – without allowing guesswork to set in, and equally importantly, to give the inexpert typist an opportunity to rectify a typographical error.

If the learner has no idea at all of the correct answer, he or she simply hits the appropriate key and is then informed of the right answer. If, however, the learner responds correctly at the first or second attempt, a congratulatory message appears, and the program moves on to the next phase.

So far, so good. Note that the learner determines the pace at which the exercise proceeds: he or she can spend a long time pondering a response or race through an exercise at breakneck speed. The learner can also abort a test at any time. More importantly even, far more opportunity for exercising an active knowledge of the language, and of receiving stimulation and encouragement (if somewhat mechanical in nature) is being provided in a few minutes' work than in several hours' contact time in a class group with a human teacher.

This system, however, does contain one apparently serious weakness: it is unable to respond flexibly if the learner offers two incorrect responses. In other words, the learner is simply told that he or she is wrong, and the correct response is offered without any explanation as to why the attempts made are wrong. You will notice that the test designer in the case of our mythical Exercise No. 99 tries to overcome this obstacle by placing a comment after the question, which points to the most common cause of error ('dreissig' is irregular in its ending), but there may indeed be other reasons which the designer has not predicted (not the least of which is faulty teaching or test design).

Given the need to keep the package as simple as possible, the solution which was adopted to meet this and other needs was to incorporate from the outset a full monitoring of student usage, recording who used the package, when, which tests were attempted, and, most importantly, which questions were answered incorrectly or not at all, and what the incorrect responses were.

In some circumstances, there may well be a case for allowing the learner to work entirely in private, as it were, but the benevolent invisible presence of Big Brother (which the students were, of course, aware of) turned out in the event to be one of the more rewarding aspects of the package, and for the very important reason that educational technology is all too often an isolated undertaking with no direct feedback into the mainstream of the teaching process, which means in addition that it is extraordinarily difficult for the package and coureseware designers to highlight weaknesses in their procedures or, for that matter, to spot particular errors made by individuals or groups of learners.

Even with a small group in the language laboratory, it is quite possible – as most readers will know all too well – for one or more learners to spend a whole class merrily reinforcing pronunciation or transformation errors if the teacher at the master console does not happen to flick the appropriate monitoring switch at precisely the right moment.

Monitoring enables the educational technology element of a course to become an integral part of that course. My colleague in Hull, Professor P. K. King, exploited this feature to the full when he bravely took up the EXERCISE package and inflicted it on his students of Dutch at beginners', intermediate and advanced levels. He divided each teaching unit into four sections:

(1) introduction of topic;
(2) language laboratory session;
(3) CALL practice; and
(4) discussion and summary.

The feedback from the monitoring output, which came in the form of a weekly armful of lineprinter output, made the fourth section particularly valuable, because it not only indicated where students tended to err (enabling better or additional exercises to be devised for present and future groups), but also highlighted where course design or teaching were deficient.

To take one simple-minded example of the latter from one of my own groups of German students, and using again the question of the German for 33: I found a number of students mistyping the German for 40, 50, and so forth, and I discovered that I had so overemphasised the exception ('drei*ss*ig', as opposed to the regular 'z' in all the others – vierzig, fünfzig, and so on) that the irregular form had superimposed itself on the others. Hence I was able to spot a general weakness in my teaching technique which I had been unaware of in the past.

By means of monitoring (sometimes called 'management' in the CALL literature) specific errors can be highlighted and particular difficulties spotted and corrected, not immediately, but within a relatively short span of time, either for the individual privately, or for the whole group if it is a more common error.

The strategy which I adopted with the CALL exercises differed quite considerably from the approach adopted for Dutch: I devised a self-contained suite of exercises which drilled both basic vocabulary and the main grammatical areas covered in the course, and the students followed these as additional material to that of the main course. After most classes, *ad hoc* exercises were devised covering specific problems which had arisen during the previous hour, and these tests proved particularly valuable in reinforcing newly-acquired knowledge.

However, this far from exhausts the complexities which flowed from my 'simple' original core design, and the lessons to be learned therefrom.

The biggest blunder which I committed, but the one from which I learned most, came with the very first exercise I devised. At that time I was a neophyte among the practitioners of CALL (if there *were* any others at that time – of that too I was ignorant), and knew nothing of the two CALL buzz-words 'linear' and 'branching'. There was, it transpired, a certain social cachet about being the proud possessor of what was called a branching program. When discussing my package, the occasional interested interlocutor, on learning that my package (despite the fact that, unlike most other packages, it was actually working in full with real live students) was merely linear, would suddenly stiffen as if there was an unpleasant odour in the room, make his excuses and depart in haste.

The blunder I had made was related indirectly to these two terms and to the ideas behind them, and it was concerned with the excessive length of the test I had devised: it contained no less than forty-eight questions to be responded to. In my innocence, that seemed to me a quite reasonable total, but after several students had been found hollow-eyed and suffering from exhaustion at the computer terminals, it rapidly became clear that CALL is a highly intensive activity, and one in which the intense degree of concentration required can be held for only a relatively brief span before tiredness sets in and the process becomes counter-effective – not least because the learner has no idea of when, if ever, he is going to finish climbing the mountain ahead.

At about this point, those terms 'linear' and 'branching' swam into my ken. A linear program offers only a single path through a test, starting at question one and proceeding in sequence to the end. A branching program, on the other

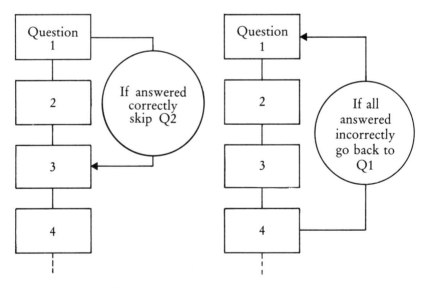

Two models for branching programs

hand, enables the designer to create multiple paths through a test, in which, for example, the better learner can be allowed to skip certain parts of the test (or be presented with more difficult questions), and the less able learner can be presented with additional back-up material. The diagram shows a couple of possible models for a branching program.

In the first model, the learner is allowed to skip past certain back-up material if the first question is answered correctly; in the second he or she is required to repeat material if it is not answered correctly. The merits or otherwise of these two approaches will be discussed in what follows.

Branching programs, so goes the sales talk, are 'flexible' and 'sensitive to the needs of the individual learner', and therefore, the syllogism concludes, they are inherently superior to linear programs.

Given the inordinate length of the first test I devised and the evidently short attention span of the learner, I went to the other extreme, breaking it up into a series of very short tests, in which the number of responses frequently did not enter double figures.

The immediate reaction of the learners was very positive: they were able to make progress in small, identifiable units, and breaking up the interaction in this way actually encouraged them to work for longer periods than they appeared to be able to cope with during the original very long test. This reaction led to the evolution of an alternative strategy to that of 'intra-program' branching, and one which I regard as superior to the well-regarded branching program for the following reasons:

(1) **Cost-effectiveness** Educational technology is a very time-consuming business, not least in the number of man-hours required to generate courseware (horror stories of hundreds of man-hours needed to produce one hour of material are not uncommon), and the clear principle that emerged from EXERCISE was that a simple test could be keyed into the computer and

debugged (checked out for errors) in a quarter of an hour or so. This is, it must be stressed, not a printing error: it is quite possible to put a dozen or so questions, answers and comments together, based on material just discussed, in little more time than it takes to put it on a scrap of paper. What the system lacked in sophistication it certainly made up for in immediacy, sensitivity to the students' needs, and effectiveness of impact. In regard to the general principle of branching and cost-effectiveness, it seemed somewhat meaningless to devise (especially *in advance* of the learners' attempting the exercise) a whole range of complex paths through an exercise, some of which may never be followed by any student at all. The prospect of debugging such a maze was also pretty daunting.

(2) **The struggling learner**   Branching cannot cope with the situation in which, even with all the help in the world, an individual learner is still floundering, even given the most supportive possible path through an exercise.

(3) **Bad educational psychology**   It is unsound, in terms of good educational psychology, to *force* a learner into a particular direction, especially when he or she might be slightly (or even more than slightly) demoralised by giving a less than brilliant performance. Given the potential for disaster that complex programming might offer, it would be even more unsound for the learner to be caught in an infinite loop, learning not how to advance his or her knowledge of a given subject, but rather how CALL packages should not be devised.

The solutions which were adopted in relation to 'branching' were as follows:

(1) A facility for the floundering student was provided by which a full listing of the questions and answers to any exercise, together with all the comments, could be requested, so that the exercise could be studied before it was undertaken. (Remarkably few students ever took up

this option, however, regarding it somehow as 'cheating', although they found it a source of comfort that it was there as a last resort.)

(2) The individual tests were designed in such a way that the concluding comment of the exercise pointed students in the direction of the next exercise in sequence; but in addition learners were advised that, if their score (given at the end of each exercise) fell below a certain level, they might like to try a revision exercise. So the option to 'branch' was retained, but the initiative was left entirely to the students. The behaviourists might baulk at the prospect of the learner having control over the progress of his or her own learning, since it is clear that the learner is not always the best judge of the level of achievement nor of the best way forward from any given point. However, this can be set against the motivational impact of putting a measure of control into the hands of the learner. In addition, this 'optional' branching enables the program to advise the learner to 'branch' into a non-computing activity if that is an appropriate option to adopt.

(3) At the end of each test, learners who had not scored 100 per cent were asked if they would like to try again those answers which had not been correctly given the first time round, and this option remained open until either all the questions had been answered correctly or the student aborted the exercise. Clearly, the danger is that the learner might be learning the sequence of responses rather than the correct answer, but that is not so likely with very short individual exercises.

(4) In addition, learners were free to repeat the same exercise as often as they wanted, although this again poses the problem of learning the sequence of the answers. Randomising (that is, reshuffling the questions into a random order, using a built-in facility) does not seem a satisfactory solution, since it would not only make the location of comments much more complex, especially

those relating to a group of questions, but also would assume that each test is a jumble of questions and answers all on the same level, with no kind of structure or organisation.

There is, however, one factor which may be regarded as less than desirable in this kind of situation. This is that, although the learner is in a less inhibiting position when guiding his or her own learning, rather than being guided by a teacher, he or she is not always the best judge of the correct approach to adopt towards the next stage in the learning process, especially when some important point has been badly understood and assimilated. Once again, it is up to the teacher to ensure that the system is properly managed and that the monitoring output is correctly evaluated. In any event, it is unlikely that any real damage is done if the CALL work is part of a well-structured overall teaching strategy.

This account of the workings and defects of the EXERCISE package has been somewhat lengthy, but should, as a case history, have pointed to the crucial problems and issues raised by CALL in general. The two important issues that remain to be explored are those of the reaction of the learners and of the way in which the package in turn should react to the learner.

5

A CALL case history II:
the learner and the machine

I spent a good deal of time observing the way in which the various groups of students reacted at the computer terminal and discussed at length with them the problems and benefits of the package. The first and most striking fact was that, after they had overcome their first nervousness at approaching the terminal (a mainframe terminal in the Applied Science building is a much more daunting prospect than a desk-top micro in the language laboratory), they soon built up a relationship with the computer. At this point I must ask the cynic to suspend disbelief, not to curl the lip in scorn: go instead to any computer centre, and you will find this happens, not just with language students running CALL packages, but with every user at all levels of ability. You will hear experienced programmers saying of the computer: 'It won't load the tapes . . . It didn't like that data . . . I couldn't get it to run that program yesterday.' Not only do computer folk discuss the machine as if it were a somewhat impractical and inconsistent colleague, they also talk to it in those terms. Go to the (somewhat unfortunately titled) terminal room, and you will find users urging the video display to 'Come on', if the delay in response time is in the user's view excessive; equally, you will find it abused as a 'Stupid machine' or grudgingly congratulated: 'At last you've got it right.'

What helps to condition this relationship is the fact that professional programmers communicate with the machine for the most part in keywords which bear some resemblance to English, and the machine responds in like terms. For example, if you go to a terminal on the DEC10 in the University of Dundee and hit the 'control' and 'C' keys simultaneously (*if* the machine is working at the time), the teletype or screen will introduce itself with a message and then invite a response: 'Please login.' The user types in his or her user number, then a password, and from then on can communicate with the monitor – say by typing 'dir' to get a listing (or 'directory' of all the relevant files), or 'debug' to run a program under the control of the delightfully named debugger. If the user makes a mistake, say by typing 'dri', the machine responds with '?dri?', indicating that communication has not been successful.

This relationship is a key element of CALL and one which should be thoroughly and properly exploited by the package designer, and it is often referred to by the dotty-sounding title of 'software psychology'. But dotty it certainly is not, especially since in language learning a relationship between student and teacher (whether human or mechanical) is crucial to the learning process, and if a relationship can be established with a mechanical tutor, then half the motivational battle has been won.

Of course the learner knows that at the other end of the line there is just an air-conditioned roomful of electronics, not a caring father figure, but equally, the learner is happy to suspend this disbelief and assume that the machine has some human characteristics. The great advantage of this game, as it were, is that the learner does not suffer from the problems of personal relationships and morale and inferiority that can so easily vitiate the learning process with a 'real' teacher. The computer is neutral but responds as if it were human. The really difficult challenge for the package designer is to exploit this pseudo-relationship.

One problem here is that there is a world of difference between a human being explaining a problem in terms that another human being can understand, and a human being 'explaining' the same problem in terms that the computer can understand.

The students responded very positively to the intense level of interaction with the computer and the constant flow of dialogue between man and machine. One of the key decisions for any courseware designer is that of achieving a correct balance between the flow of information from the computer, requiring passive reading from the learner, and, on the other hand, the positive input from the learner.

It appeared also that the physical involvement in the act of typing enhanced levels of concentration and motivation, although both were offset to a small extent in the early stages by some students who found it irksome to come to terms with a QWERTY keyboard. In those instances, the irritation was a passing phenomenon, and students were overwhelmingly pleased to have an opportunity to acquire even a two-fingered typing skill.

Involvement with keyboard and screen overcame one major problem posed by the language laboratory, namely, sensory deprivation. In many language lab learning situations, there is nothing much for the hands to do (except press the 'play', 'recap', and 'stop' buttons) and nothing at all for the eyes. Not only did the computer overcome this problem (although care must be taken to ensure that the overall lighting conditions do not induce eyestrain, and there are of course the occasional medical problems in which it is inadvisable for the patient to look at a TV screen at all), a new element rapidly emerged without prompting by the teacher. Students were observed to gather spontaneously into groups of three or four round a single terminal, and to engage in animated discussion, partly about problems of communicating with the machine, but mainly about the actual language work being tested. This again contrasts with most language laboratory work, in which students typically sit in isolation.

Encouraging learners to discuss their problems in the controlled conditions of a CALL test can do nothing but good, and produces a welcome shift of the initiative in the learning process from teacher to learner. As has been pointed out earlier, there are problems in allowing the learner a measure of control over learning patterns and strategies, but here as elsewhere the advantages far outweigh the difficulties. The most important of the advantages is the heightened motivation together with the ability to share difficulties with fellow learners and articulate problems which in a class situation tend to remain unspoken and misunderstood.

One curious phenomenon of software psychology which puzzled me considerably when first I encountered it was an odd kind of assumption which the learner made about the computer. It soon transpired that it is a situation common to all naive computer users and poses quite difficult problems for the package designer. What happened was that I had at one stage inadvertently introduced a bug into the EXERCISE package when I was modifying the CALL program within the package. What was supposed to happen was that, at the end of an exercise, the program would work out if the learner had got all the responses correct, and, if the score was not perfect, offer the opportunity for incorrect responses to be tried again. Unfortunately, I had succeeded in causing the program to terminate whether the score was 100 per cent or not.

The puzzling feature of this situation was that the error went entirely unreported, and it was only purely by chance that I discovered it. (To my embarrassment, it was in the course of an on-line demonstration at another university!) When I discussed the problem with the students who were regularly trying the CALL exercises, they confirmed that they too had noted the aberration, and that it was a cause for concern, but they assumed that the machine had by some means and for its own reasons 'decided' to modify its normal practice.

This reaction is very similar to that of the unpractised computer user who in error or in ignorance keys in an inaccurate or inapposite sequence of characters, receives an error message, but who persists in typing exactly the same sequence several times over in the hope and expectation that, somehow, it will finally dawn on the computer what the user is trying to communicate.

6

Authoring packages

This is a survey of current packages available on computing for language teachers and of how interested readers can break into the magic circle of computer jargon and either become their own programmers or, at the least, use packages devised by others to experiment with their own courseware. The objective is to provide representative information and guidance rather than the kind of exhaustive and exhausting comprehensiveness that an academic study of this field would call for, since a great deal of work, if not actually duplicating, overlaps considerably.

In the old mainframe days, CALL – where it existed – was the exclusive preserve of a few privileged beings in higher education, who were, in the considered view of their colleagues, not entirely in possession of their proper senses. Having said that, it must be admitted that the EXERCISE package, written for the Hull mainframe and described in the two preceding chapters, attracted considerable positive interest once the barriers of incomprehension and suspicion were overcome, and a straw poll of other pioneers in the field indicates that their experiences were not vastly different. The problem which arose subsequently was to exploit the enthusiasm of new converts and enable them to advance from the stage of initial enthusiasm to the point at which they might perform some courseware design of their own, and one possible way of making this step forward was the bought-in package.

Most of these authoring packages were originally designed for complex, expensive mainframe systems, but some have either been rewritten for the micro or specially written for that environment.

There are a number of such packages in existence, most bearing the compulsory tortuous acronymic title. One such is PILOT (Programmed Instruction Learning Or Teaching), most familiar in the version designed for the Apple micro-computer. PLATO (Programmed Logic for Automatic Teaching Operation) was originally designed at the University of Illinois, and is now marketed by Control Data Corporation. This is a microcomputer version, but has the distinct drawback of being available only on special disks which have to be purchased from the manufacturer, and this severely limits their availability. Wise (manufactured by Wicat, the World Institute for Computer Aided Teaching) makes particular claims for its graphic capabilities, but is essentially a mainframe package.

Kosmos Software offer packages for French, German, and Spanish, which allow the creation of simple question and answer exercises as well as offering a large number of built-in exercises (BBC micro and Spectrum). TES/T (Tandberg Educational Software/Testing, copyright Tandberg Ltd), designed by the present author, is targeted on to the CP/M micro and the BBC micro. Questionmaster (formerly known as Teacher's Toolkit), designed originally for the Pet microcomputer by Graham Davies, is now published by Hutchinson Software. Both TES/T and Questionmaster have useful and informative manuals describing their features and design philosophy. EDUTEXT comes from the National Physical Laboratory, Middlesex, UK, and has a version for the micro called MICROTEXT. This system, which is claimed to be highly sophisticated, very flexible and which in some versions can cope with videodiscs and other peripherals, is shortly to become available on a number of popular micros. TICCIT (Time-shared Interactive Computer-Controlled Information Television) was developed at Brigham Young University and is now owned by Hazeltine, but that, too, is a mainframe system, as is EXTOL (East Anglia and Essex

Teaching-Oriented Languages), designed to facilitate the creation of drilling exercises and the like.

From this list, I select one representative example of the authoring packages which require the learning of a language, however simple, in order to be able to set up and run exercises on the computer, and three from those which do not require the learning of any language. All four examples selected are available in the micro environment.

PILOT is designed to cope with question and answer sequences, and a micro with at least one disk drive is essential if the system is not to be impossibly slow. This is not the place for a comprehensive programming manual of PILOT (you would have to turn to the Apple PILOT Manual for that). What follows is a description of the main features of the language.

PILOT is based on a sequence of commands, abbreviated to initial letters followed by a colon. Hence R: stands for Remark (that is, a comment for the benefit of the exercise compiler), T: for Type Text, A: for Accept Input from the learner, and so on.

Modifiers allow the user to vary the significance of the operating codes. For example M:, which stands for Match with input (in other words, M: is followed by the model response which is to be compared with what the learner now types in as his or her attempt at the correct answer), can be modified with an S. MS: means allow certain slight spelling variations in the response to be regarded as correct.

Conditioners enable the programmer to take different courses of action depending on the response from the learner and to accept a variety of different responses.

Variables may be assigned values and various other functions can be set (for example, converting all input to upper and/or lower case).

A brief sample of a PILOT session might go something like this, and should be self-explanatory. The test designer would type in these instructions to the computer:

T: This is a demonstration
T: What is two plus two?
A:
M: four ! 4 ! iv
R: The ! = 'or'
TY: Aren't you a clever thing?
TN: Can't you even add to four?

Briefly interpreted: the first two lines are text, which is printed on to the screen when the exercise is summoned up by the learner. Then the computer waits to accept a response to the question from the learner; and if that response is four, 4 or iv, as the remark in the next line explains, the text for the right answer (TY: – text if yes) is printed, otherwise the text for the wrong answer appears on the screen.

That taste of the commands employed by PILOT might well frighten the life out of any reader who is keen to explore computers in CALL but has never yet actually met a micro in the flesh. However, learning PILOT is not a horrendously difficult exercise, and I have seen a group of teachers acquire a very basic level of skill in PILOT in the course of a couple of hours at the micro.

The trouble with PILOT is that, even given a sympathetic teacher and an aptitude for computing on the part of the novice, it is no trivial matter for the complete computer novice to attain a reasonable level of competence without the investment of a fair amount of effort and in many cases the absorption of a measure of culture shock. And, as has been stressed already, it is not simply a matter of acquiring the skill to 'program' the computer.

Learning to program even in a straightforward authoring language is rather like trying to learn to drive a car. It would be all nice and easy if one could concentrate on steering first, then on the brakes, then on the gear changes, and so on, but some level of awareness of a whole range of skills is required from the outset: how to insert a disk, how to correct typing errors, how to load the package, what techniques to employ in the presentation of material on the screen, what range of optional responses to permit, and so on. And once the investment of time and effort in achieving a modest level of competence has been made, it is somewhat galling – to return to the vehicular metaphor – to discover that one has learned to drive a car with only one forward gear and no lights for driving in the dark.

In other words, PILOT is a self-contained system which does not permit the user either to extend its potential range or to turn it away from the question-and-answer approach. As in so much CALL, good or bad, the problem of overcoming the limitations of a particular piece of software presents the user with the need to expend what may well appear to be a disproportionate amount of effort in aquiring new skills in order to take the next step forward.

There are also technical problems in the current version of Apple PILOT which cause the disk access times to be slow, and as a result the learner has to wait for a perceptible and irritating amount of time for his or her responses to be processed and acted upon.

PILOT is frustrating to the very kind of teacher who is attracted to CALL in the first place, for the following reason. It requires some effort to overcome initial familiarisation problems; but, once these problems have been overcome, frustration at the limitations of the package leads to a curiosity as to what alternatives there are, and the answer to this is to learn a 'real' programming language (of which more in a moment). At this point the aggrieved enthusiast asks, not without some justification, why he or she was not given the chance of so doing in the first instance.

Worst of all, PILOT can tend to restrict the user to one particular kind of strategy, the conversational or tutorial approach, in other words that of question and answer, a dialogue between learner and machine based on right and wrong responses. Although even a limited system such as this can – as I hope I demonstrated in the case of the EXERCISE package above – be of value in the learning of languages, it has two disadvantages. It presents the teacher with a very restricted conception of the potential of the micro in CALL; and it can also lead the unwary, as happened all too often in the case of the language laboratory, to adopt teaching strategies suited to the hardware rather than to exploit the technology in ways suited to his or her particular aims and approach.

Having said that, PILOT has its strong supporters as well as its detractors (those anxious, perhaps, to drop the PILOT), and the amount of interest it has generated in the computing press indicates that serious CALL users should at least consider the possibility of programming some of their material in that language, provided of course that a version exists for the machine to which access is available.

An alternative strategy to adopt is to try in the first instance a menu-driven package which requires no knowledge of any programming. Such no-code authoring systems, as they are called, do exist, and I turn now briefly to three of them, Kosmos Software's package, Questionmaster, and TES/T.

Of these packages, the simplest in concept is that offered by Kosmos. It is a straightforward question-and-answer sequence with a couple of nice features, very simple to use or create exercises with, and able to cope with the appropriate foreign accents, etc. The package is available in French, German and Spanish versions. Each package comes with 32 ready-made lessons, and lesson creation and editing routines. The first lesson in each language, for example, contains vocabulary relating to the family and progresses through the whole range of basic vocabulary, culminating in adjectives, adverbs, and verb forms. These lessons can be added to by means of a simple routine.

Each lesson can be run in one of two modes, either a preview mode, in which the questions and answers are shown on the screen for a predetermined number of seconds, or learners can test themselves (in both cases, the lesson can be from or into the foreign language). In the testing mode, the learner is offered help one letter at a time, but there are no facilities for branching, prompting, reinforcement or random access to the questions and answers.

It is possible to confuse the package by wilful mistyping, but it offers in general terms a very unpretentious introduction for both teacher and learner to tutorial-type CALL. It is the kind of package which gets a bad reception from those who fancy themselves to be at the sharp end of research in this field, but which the teacher trying to come to terms with CALL and many learners will find both straightforward and attractive.

Questionmaster is altogether more ambitious. This, like the TES/T package, is an 'empty box' package, and it requires that you specify in advance the number of questions you wish to incorporate into an exercise. For each question and answer, a maximum of eight lines is allowed, and the number has to be specified in advance. Help notes can be provided for the learner.

First, the exercise creator is asked to type an introduction to the exercise. Then the question-and-answer sequence is typed in; comments are allowed for questions and for incorrect responses. A number of alternative answers are permitted, which can be in hierarchical form, the best answer first. Upper case conversion of characters is allowed, and the test can be divided into a number of blocks of questions and answers. Remedial reruns of tests can also be permitted. The package is accompanied by a well-written handbook (published by Hutchinson Software, 1982), which contains useful pieces of practical advice.

The TES/T package is the most complicated of the trio, and it enables the non-computing expert to design a tutorial-type test, a presentation of material, or a combination of both (with the option of audio back-up, for which see Chapter 8). The notion behind the design, which grew out of EXERCISE, is not only to permit the production of courseware, but also to allow teachers to experiment with aspects of CALL without having to commit themselves to learning a programming or authoring language.

In the BBC Micro version of the package, the teacher is presented with a menu of options (creating, editing, listing, copying, renaming, erasing, or running a test). In the creation mode, the teacher is first invited to inspect and/or alter the options available: these include the facility to alter the number of attempts the learner is permitted; to show the shape of the answer as a pattern of X's; to split the screen, with the result that the upper half of the screen is retained whilst the lower half can be changed, thus allowing paradigms or instructions to be kept in front of the learner; and so forth.

In Mode 7 (Teletext) colour text and graphics are available. In Mode 6, a feature enables text to be typed on alternate lines, with extra-clear accents appearing above the characters. The BBC's character generator is less than satisfactory for the circumflex, let alone upper case characters with accents.

All the options can be changed at any time during the creation of a test. When these have been inspected, the teacher is presented with a blank screen on to which he or she can type his or her material, using the cursor keys to move around the screen. If a question and answer are required, the latter is typed in double quotation marks – there are special arrangements for long answers – something like this (the sentence translates as 'The young man goes into the classroom'):

Der junge Mann geht "ins" Klassenzimmer.

When the learner is running the program, the 'ins' disappears, and the cursor is placed in the appropriate location after 'geht'. The response is then typed in by the learner (there is a feature to prevent over-typing of 'Klassenzimmer'), who is able to delete individual characters or the whole response. Simply hitting the 'return' key indicates that he or she has no idea of the correct response. After responding, the learner has the option of exiting at any time from the test.

Those readers familiar with German will be asking themselves about the contracted form of the pronoun plus definite article; what if the learner types 'in das', which is equally correct? Facilities exist for alternative answers, and too for 'wild cards', which can stand for individual characters or strings of characters.

When a screenful of text and/or graphics is completed to the satisfaction of the teacher, he or she is invited to put up another screenful of information and questions and answers, inspect or change the options, invoke reinforcement and/or branching, or end the test.

In reinforcing and branching, the test designer can activate the routines if the learner gives (a) the correct answer; (b) the wrong answer; (c) any answer; or (d) a specified answer. A learner, for example, who types 'im' or 'in dem', can be reminded with a screenful of information that this is a preposition which requires the accusative where change of state or movement is involved, or can be branched to a set of back-up questions (or, indeed, both).

The above is intended to do no more than give a flavour of a no-code authoring package. One additional feature which has not been referred to is the ability to connect the micro to a computer-controlled random access tape recorder, thus adding sound to vision. (This will be discussed in Chapter 8.)

For many users, PILOT, TES/T, Questionmaster, or one of the other packages may well satisfy most needs; but what if, appetite whetted, a teacher is led by enthusiasm to seek to explore beyond the limits, however apparently flexible, which others have set in the design of these packages?

The trouble with all packages is that they determine what you can do; very few can allow the programmer to extend the features of the package or incorporate his or her own code. For the adventurous there is no real option but to take up a programming language.

And that has to mean BASIC. This language, for all its age and defects, is the most commonly available on nearly all micros, and indeed the only language available on some, and in its better versions does offer a reasonable approach to programming. Ideally, other languages more suitable for linguistic programming should be employed; unfortunately, they have yet to be designed.

This is not the place for a BASIC programming manual – there are far too many of them around already – but the language can be mastered in a relatively short time by anyone with programming aptitude; and if you can learn a foreign language a programming language should hold no terrors, since it is an artificial language, constructed according to unambiguous rules of grammar and syntax, with mnemonics and English-like constructions (for example, IF . . . THEN . . . ELSE) to make programming itself easier. It must not be thought that the programmer should be a mathematics expert, since the kind of programming required does not involve any more than the most elementary arithmetic, and even assembly language only requires the ability to work in hexadecimal (which is no insuperable problem for those used to operating to the base 16 in weighing ounces and pounds). Besides, the micro can be persuaded to act in what is known as 'immediate mode' as a calculator whenever arithmetic rears its ugly head.

Programming is much more concerned with logic than with arithmetic and can provide for the language teacher with the appropriate aptitude a fascinating extension of existing skills and expertise, quite regardless of its practical value in the classroom for CALL work.

7

CALL in practice: from off-the-peg to do-it-yourself

We now consider examples of off-the-peg and DIY CALL across the whole range of applications. The objective is to be representative rather than comprehensive, and where any one application is traceable back to an originator, the name and institution are given. These are generalised accounts which do not necessarily reflect in detail what individual researchers have done. The aim is to provide a broad picture of current work on CALL without becoming anecdotal or merely cataloguing. There is no attempt to 'classify' these illustrations in any particular order of merit, only into broad categories of program.

Attempts have been made by others at a taxonomy of CALL, in which programs have been divided into three types: analytic, tutorial, and synthetic. The differences between these categories are often more apparent than real, however, and with the exception of the synthetic programs, which do form a genuine group on their own, the examples enumerated in this chapter have been divided according to the kind of programming involved or the particular aspect or aspects of the computer which are employed.

What emerges is a strikingly diverse pattern of usage, in which the ability of the micro to match strings of characters naturally plays an important role, but so too does the ability to manipulate text, store and retrieve information, move text about the screen, draw pictures in colour, control external devices – in fact, there is hardly a single aspect of the micro which has not been exploited by researchers in this field. At the end of the chapter a number of general conclusions which derive from the descriptions of CALL applications are drawn together in an attempt to enunciate a set of broad principles for the use of the micro in language teaching by both the programmer and user.

Although references are largely to modern language teaching, the English and EFL teacher will readily recognise that all the programs described can profitably be applied to their disciplines, and that in fact they are particularly well served by general off-the-peg material, such as word processing packages and computer games. I am not attempting to discriminate against the English and EFL teacher; but the fact is that until very recently the overwhelming majority of CALL work has been done in the field of modern language teaching.

(1) Question and answer

As you will have gathered, this application is much despised by those who, rightly rejecting the Skinnerian approach of programmed learning, have wrongly thrown out the baby with the bathwater by rejecting any form of tutorial program which is based on question and answer. If it is recognised that drilling in isolation is not the happiest way of acquiring lexical competence, and too that question and answer programs are at their best when part of an overall teaching strategy rather than as an isolated hole-in-the-corner activity, then such programs will find a positive and valuable place in CALL applications.

One of the greatest advantages of the question-and-answer approach is that the programming skills required to match a response with the model are modest; and that is also one of the greatest disadvantages too, since most budding CALL programmers set off with an ill thought-out routine which is then demonstrated to a group of cynics who condemn it, and by implication all question-and-answer programs and CALL in its entirety. The programming may be fairly simple, but a great deal of thought has to be devoted to designing a format which does not lead the learner astray, as was demonstrated above in relation to the EXERCISE package.

Once properly written, the most positive aspect of such programs is that they are context-free and as such a very cost-effective means of applying the micro to language teaching. All that is required in the simplest version is the following sequence:

(1) identification and introduction to the test;
(2) a sequence of questions and answers;
(3) clues where appropriate;
(4) reinforcement of correct and incorrect responses.

This program enables the teacher to design material with the minimum of computing effort. All that is needed is some care in laying out the screen and in coping with varying responses from the learner.

The simplest form of the question-and-answer approach is a vocabulary test, usually in the form of a translation: 'What is the German/French/Spanish etc. for the following word?' It is perhaps because this is the most obvious application and the simplest by far to put together that the most ghastly examples of how not to program have been seen here. As was discussed earlier in the case of the EXERCISE package, it is far from simple to design effective routines to overcome problems such as the need for learners to include or omit the definite article in their responses, the issue of alternative answers, the number of attempts allowed, the presentation of clues, the correct way of reinforcing wrongly answered questions (not just by telling learners they are wrong and giving the right answer), and so forth.

It is in this area that a little imagination can overcome the limitations of this kind of routine, for example, by simply telling the learner not to incorporate the article or by giving clues to the answer. Objections to teaching lexis can readily be overcome by presenting the answer in the context of a couple of sentences which demonstrate its use. Other variants can be employed, for example, presenting the learner with a graphic representation of the object for which the French or German is to be offered (after all, most vocabulary learning in the native language at the earlier stages is done not by saying 'Here is the word DOG, learn it' but by 'Look, doggie').

The problem of a learner simply learning the order in which the responses come rather than the responses themselves (most frequently seen in the context of the times tables) can be overcome by 'shuffling' the order of answers using the random number generator of the micro (ensuring, of course, that you do not follow the same pseudo-random sequence on each and every occasion!), unless there is a clear progression in the exercise.

An attractive variation on the question-and-answer type of program is the 'slot-filling' exercise, which exploits the fact that text can be located on the screen under the control of the micro. The learner can be asked to provide the correct form of the verb by typing in the response at the appropriate point in the sentence, for example: 'Il . . . le chocolat (aimer).' In this kind of situation it is useful to employ the technique of splitting the screen: the upper half presents the paradigm and a couple of examples; the lower half only of the screen changes with each question and answer.

One of the most useful applications of the question-and-answer type of exercise is the transformational test, which many learners find difficult to master. The learner is invited to answer questions on the model: 'Are you working hard?' The response might be 'Yes, I am working hard', or 'No, I am not working hard.'

Another valuable application is in the field of word order, which presents the learner with many problems. Two programs designed to test some aspects of this subject are discussed below in relation to graphics and animation, but even a simple test on these lines can both encourage the learner to overcome his or her difficulties, and has the merit of not requiring the learner to type in anything more complicated than single digits. The output on the screen might look something like this, with double spacing to indicate clearly where each section begins and ends:

1	2	3	4
Der Mann	geht	jeden Tag	in die Stadt.

The learner is invited to type the digits corresponding to the correct order if 'Jeden Tag' comes at the beginning of the sentence (that is, 3 – 2 – 1 – 4), and the program will then display the text in the correct order. This is a straightforward program to write, and can be easily generalised to cope with other issues such as subordination in German or negation in French. Help information can be provided for the learner in difficulties. (In the graphics and animation section below a more sophisticated variant on this program is described, as is the technique for rearranging the text on the screen.)

The variations that can be played on the simple question-and-answer model are legion: multiple choice can easily be accommodated into the model, so long as the limitations of this technique are recognised, as can reading comprehension tests, asking the learner to insert punctuation or unscramble word order, and so on.

(2) Sentence building

A powerful application, far removed from the drilling and testing which formed the basis of our case history and the last section, has been demonstrated by Tony Crispin, of the Scottish Curriculum Development Centre. It is aimed at the beginner and/or the learner who is experiencing difficulty in constructing continuous discourse in the foreign language. The application has the additional merit of not just being an exercise for its own sake; there is a positive spin-off for the learner.

The learner is posed a number of personal questions by the computer (let us say, in French), which asks name, sex, age, address, and a number of other questions relating to family, home, and interests. When the sequence of questions is complete, the program generates on the screen a letter in French based on the answers to the questions, which can serve as a basis for a first letter to a pen friend in the foreign country. The practical difficulties which may be encountered include devising means of preventing learners from playing the fool, introducing themselves as Mickey Mouse or Adolf Hitler with impossibly large families and somewhat unorthodox pastimes. Surprisingly, it seems that the imagination of the potential blasphemer is pretty limited, and it is not too difficult to incorporate routines to flush out all but the most ingenious malingerer.

Such an exercise could be dry as dust, but it is enlivened by some simple but effective touches from its author. At the beginning of the routine, for example, a simple representation of a blindfolded face appears on the screen. Beneath it are the words in the appropriate language: 'I can't see. Are you a boy or a girl?'

The two chief educational objections to this kind of program are, first, that it may be regarded not as a stage in the acquisition of fluency but as an alternative to, or a means of avoiding, such progress. This, however, is a matter for the skill of the teacher; it is not an inherent weakness in the program. The second objection, which again is not the fault of the program, but a general problem facing the pioneers of CALL, is that the learner will be able to complete the letter-writing program in ten minutes at the very most – and then will be demanding similar exercises, possibly becoming mildly disillusioned with the micro on learning that it will be a considerable while before more programs are developed.

(3) Graphics and animation

The ability to move the cursor about the screen on the micro can be used to considerable effect in demonstration routines of, for example, German word order, or the proper sequence for French pronouns. This involves a higher level of programming expertise, but the effectiveness of this technique is very considerable; in addition, it is one of the applications of the micro in which one machine can be used with a whole class of learners as a kind of electronic blackboard.

The core of the technique is as follows: take, for example, the German sentence 'Wir fahren morgen nach London' (We are going to London tomorrow). In English, the reversal of word order results in a 'shunt' of words down the sentence: 'Tomorrow we are going to London.' In German, however, the sentence pivots round the verb, which retains its second place: 'Morgen fahren wir nach London.' This is not easy for the learner to comprehend, but a demonstration program which shows the words actually moving round the screen, particularly in conjunction with colour changes, brings home to the learner the concept of the main clause verb in German as 'second idea'. In addition, the same program can readily be adapted to accept input from the learner, so that he or she can watch his or her own sentence move round the screen, and relatively slight modifications to the program can be introduced to demonstrate what happens in German when a main clause becomes a subordinate clause.

The programming technique involves splitting the sentence into its component parts: (1) subject ('wir'), (2) tensed verb ('fahren'), (3) qualifier ('morgen'), (4) rest of main clause ('nach London'). The sentence is displayed on the screen in this order, then a routine is invoked to move (3) up the screen, across to the lefthand side of the screen and in front of (1); then (1) and (2) are interchanged.

To explain in a little more detail; if you assume that the plus sign indicates that the text strings are joined together, the original sentence looks like this: 'wir' + 'fahren' + 'morgen' + 'nach' + 'London'. A space after each word prevents the words from running into one another on the screen. This information is placed on the screen, with two modifications: a full stop is placed at the end, and the first letter of the first string is converted to an upper case character if necessary: 'Wir'. Then the string containing 'morgen' is replaced by seven spaces (= the length of 'morgen' plus the trailing space)

and the word is printed on the line above the text on the
screen preceded by eleven spaces (= the length of the
preceding words and spaces). 'morgen' is printed on the next
line up and the line below is cleared. This process is repeated
for a couple of lines until the text looks like this:

← ——— morgen

Wir fahren   nach London.

Then the 'wir' is moved downwards by the same technique,
and the 'morgen' moved across to the left as the 'wir' is
moved to the right. The position of 'fahren' is adjusted to
account for the fact that 'morgen' is longer than 'wir', and the
two words are then raised/lowered into their new locations.
'morgen' acquires a capital initial letter, and the process is
complete. Even the non-programmer will see that this
process can readily be generalised to cope with different
vocabulary, once the techniques involved have been mastered.

There is one potential weakness in this kind of routine,
which emerges if one moves one element all the way before
readjusting the sequencing. In other words, the following
will appear on the screen for a moment: 'morgen wir fahren
nach London' before 'morgen' is moved. It is as bad practice
on the electronic blackboard as it is on its chalky predecessor
to present the learner with incorrect material.

A similar program which I have written demonstrates and
tests the use of French object pronouns, which cause a
number of problems to the learner, both because these
pronouns are located between subject and verb in contrast to
English practice, and also because they follow a predetermined sequence.

A sample sentence is put up on the screen (let us say, 'Il
donne du pain à son frère'); the latter part of the sentence is
moved up the screen; 'en' and 'lui' are placed above the 'du
pain' and 'à son frère' respectively; then the two are
transposed into the correct order: 'lui en'. The 'donne' moves

to the right, leaving an appropriate gap for the 'lui en' to shuffle across and drop into the middle; 'Il lui en donne' then appears; and at this point the option exists for negating the sentence, changing the tense, and introducing the positive and negative forms of the imperative.

After a demonstration, the option exists for the learner to test him or herself or for the teacher to put up another demonstration on to the screen. In self-testing and demonstrating, the program has to be smart enough to cope with 'J'aime la fleur' changing and eliding to 'Je l'aime', but it was not felt to be cost-effective to allow for h-aspirates!

It is important that dedicated programs like those just described should exploit their potential to the full: it is no trivial matter to create a generalised set of procedures to move chunks of text of varying lengths round the screen, especially given the need to swap round 'en' and 'lui' and other pronominal forms, and, too, to cope with eliding. The best solution to the problem of cost-effectiveness that I have found is to allow the program to operate in more than one mode: demonstration, which enables the computer to be used as an electronic animated blackboard for the whole class or for the individual learner, and testing, in this case based on a randomly accessed collection of verbs and nouns with their accompanying pronouns. So one program can be applied in different modes, and integrated into the total learning pattern in a much more effective manner than if it were sitting in a corner waiting for the casual self-access learner to appear.

Graphics and animation can be employed in a variety of other ways, one of the commonest of which is the presentation of a map on the screen. The learner is invited to find the way to the town hall or station by issuing instructions to the computer (to turn right, left, or go straight ahead). A map of a shopping centre can be put up on the screen, and the learner asked where it is possible to buy bread, meat, or newspapers. Or again, the learner can be invited to place the names of towns or rivers on a map, or put names to objects on the screen (in a room, the window, door, table, television, and so forth). The questioning technique can be varied to suit the level of ability and knowledge of the learner. The beginner or less able can be required only to type a digit to correspond to the correct location on the screen; for example, if the butcher's shop is numbered 3 on the map, the response need only be the appropriate digit, whereas the more advanced learner might be required to type in a complete sentence.

The outline drawing of a room can be further exploited in the context of testing prepositions. The learner can either be invited to indicate where a particular object is ('Où est le chat?'), or in a variation on this theme, the learner can be invited to place the cat on the mat or elsewhere in the room. Another variation is to hide an object and ask the learner to guess where it is. This encourages practice of a simple dialogue: 'Is the cat behind the television? . . . No, it is not there. Try somewhere else.' In this kind of test, the programmer can determine whether at one level the learner has to type in a full question, or at a more elementary level is simply required to key the number of an object in, after first being told that the cat is hidden behind one of the objects on the screen.

Yet another variation on this theme is to invite the learner to fill a house with items of furniture. 'Here is a television. Where shall I put it?' might be the initial impetus from the computer, with a ground plan of the house on the screen.

The screen can also be used as an oscilloscope, demonstrating the way in which sounds can appear, and enabling the learner to imitate the model on the screen. This requires sophisticated equipment, but it is an excellent method of instructing learners who either have hearing problems or are seeking to acquire verbal competence in a language like Chinese where pitch is significant to meaning.

(4) **Filling in gaps**
This is quite different from the 'slot-filling' tests discussed above, and has become very popular indeed in CALL circles, so much so that it is invidious to isolate any one program.

The theoretical basis of what is called the clozentropy exercise can be divided into two parts: on the one hand it is concerned with guessing strategy, or inferencing ability to give it its alternative name, on the other with enabling individual attempts at responses to be compared with the responses of others in the group, with the response being scored according to what proportion of the group has decided on the same answer (a procedure which can bristle with horrendous pitfalls in language teaching).

As all the clozentropy-type exercises on the micro that I have encountered concentrate exclusively on the former aspect and have ignored the latter, I have called this group of programs gapping tests. Guessing strategy is a much under-used aspect of language learning, and to combine it as in these tests with an emphasis on the context as a whole makes it a very desirable learning tool.

What typically happens in a computerised gapping test is that a text is displayed on the screen, but at predetermined regular intervals a word is omitted. The task of the learner is to fill in the gaps with the correct word. This exercise both improves the learner's awareness of the total context of a linguistic situation, and also enhances his or her guessing strategy. It has the additional advantage, in selecting words for omission at regular intervals, of testing a whole range of different linguistic skills, rather than homing in exclusively on, say, verbal forms.

The text must, of course, be selected with a measure of prudence, to avoid situations in which the learner is faced with a gap which can be filled with, say, one of a range of synonyms, or a manufacturer's trade mark which cannot be deduced from the context, or again an elided or hyphenated word.

The gapping test has the great advantage of extreme flexibility of presentation. The interval between gaps can be varied under learner or teacher control and the learner can fill in the gaps in random order. Clues can be given, either by indicating the length of the word omitted, or by giving its initial letter or letters; and, if a learner's attempt at filling a gap is only partially successful, the program can indicate the letters correctly guessed (making it a kind of 'hangman' game plus context).

In addition, other options can be offered. A more sophisticated database might include alternative words at appropriate points, or incorporate a facility for feeding back to the teacher the incorrect responses. The criteria for blanking out words can be modified to depend, not on the number of words given between blanked-out words, but rather on criteria such as word length (all words over four letters in length might be blanked out); words in a look-up table might be omitted – for example, all forms of the auxiliaries 'sein', 'haben', and 'werden' in German; or words containing particular prefixes or suffixes can be blanked out, such as words ending in 'ing' in English, or the inseparable verbal prefixes in German.

Alternatively, the missing word can be presented in the form of an anagram. Or again, the whole screen can be initially blanked out, allowing the learner to progress only in sequence and to base the answers solely on the information preceding the current gap to be filled, or permitting the learner to guess the words or letters in words at random. A variation on this last approach is to show the whole text for a predetermined time, as indicated in the section on memory tests above, and then show it as a sequence of dashes and spaces only on the screen. The learner can then try to recall the text, and each time a word is correctly recalled, it is placed in its proper location on the screen, with each occurrence of the word shown. This would enable the learner to start off with the obvious candidates for inclusion, such as definite and indefinite articles, prepositions, and so forth.

The gapping test is an ideal exercise to be undertaken by a group of learners, thus both extending computer access and, more importantly, rendering the analysis of the text a common rather than, as so often in linguistic exercises, an isolated activity.

Completing the circle, as it were, it is simple to incorporate a monitoring facility for the same reasons as in the EXERCISE project discussed above: to check on the quality of the data and the performance of the learner; and to enable the teacher to make the data more relevant to the needs of the learners.

(5) **Memory tests**

There are a number of variations which can be played on this notion: either a list of names or a piece of text can be placed on the screen for a specified time, then removed, and the learners invited to reconstruct what they have seen. The game which allows the players to see objects on a tray for a certain time, then has them list as many as they remember, can easily be created on the micro, with variations such as the computer asking: 'Was there a box of matches on the tray?' or 'How many books were on the tray?'

(6) **Using the word processor**

First, a paragraph which can be skipped by those familiar with the workings of a word processor.

Put simply, a word processor is – among other things – a means of using the computer as a glorified typewriter. The great disadvantage of typing is that, once text has been committed to paper, it is far from easy to modify anything but the most trivial typographical errors, let alone reorganise the text, cut out or insert paragraphs, justify right and left, and so on. Such procedures are greatly facilitated by the computer. Text can be typed directly on to the screen and held in the computer's memory, and it is simplicity itself to rearrange and reorganise the material typed in, as it is to search for specified characters in the text. The final stage is to list the text on an output device such as a daisywheel or matrix printer, with page numbering, running heads, right justification, and a whole range of other options.

Computing purists may well object that to use the word processor for CALL purposes is a trivial application of the computer; trivial or not, that kind of argument is quite irrelevant. Whether or not the computer is being used in a way which exploits the whole of its potential, the validity of any application should be judged on its own merits. It is no 'waste' of a colour micro with high-resolution graphics to use it for black-and-white typing on to the screen. The greatest advantage of word processor packages is that they are already written and can be bought off the shelf: there is no programming to be done, and the awkward question of the absence of good-quality software does not apply. All the learner has to do is to get to know the way in which the word processor operates, and most such packages are specifically designed for the non-expert user and contain full support and explanatory facilities.

(a) *Translation exercises:* Derek Lewis in the Department of Modern Languages at Dundee University, Scotland, has been experimenting with the word processor to enable the learner to be more flexible in approaching what has always been a daunting exercise. The source language is keyed in in advance, with large gaps between the lines, and the learner is invited to key in his or her version in the gaps. The advantages of this approach are as follows: the learner can be encouraged to work outwards from the easier sections of the exercises, rather than starting at the beginning and switching in a disorganised fashion from writing to dictionary searching and grammar checking; the search facilities enable checking and comparison to be carried out easily; and the ease with which text on the screen can be modified encourages experimentation.

(b) *Note-taking:* One of the more difficult skills to acquire for the more advanced school learner or the college student is that of being able to take notes either from books and articles or from lectures and seminars. It is one of those skills which it is far from easy to teach, not least because the needs of individual learners and their retention abilities vary considerably. The only way to learn is to do it, and this can mean the poor student having to cope with assimilating new material and learning how to take notes on it at the same time.

Given the word processor, the learner can practise note-taking and can correct the material under supervision in a manner impossible with pen and paper. The final version can then be printed and filed for future reference.

(c) *Writing an essay:* This is a project currently being undertaken in the Modern Languages Department, University of Dundee, by Rex Last and Derek Lewis. One of the central problems confronting the teacher of compositional skills (that is, if those skills are actually taught properly) is that of coping with the transfer between what might be termed the 'random access' and 'linear' phases of the exercise.

To explain: the model for an essay is set out in the diagram, together with the all too frequent reality:

	Model	Common pattern
Introduction		
Central section		
Conclusion		

The learner tends to deviate increasingly from the model in progressing through the essay. Usually the introduction is moderately substantial, although it can tend to suffer either from being too remote from the subject at hand ('Throughout the long history of Western civilisation we can see that . . .'), or from closing myopically in on the topic from the opening sentence ('I believe *Hamlet* to be a tragedy because . . .'). The central section, in which the arguments are developed, tends to be lopsided, with the most important points placed first, and tailing off into whatever else the learner happens to remember. The conclusion, if there is one, is frequently a one-line restatement of the theme of the essay ('Thus I think that *Hamlet* is a tragedy.').

Overstatement this may be, but it is a fairly accurate composite of what happens time and again in essays at school and university level. The real tragedy is that the weaknesses lie not so much in the learner as in the technology he or she is obliged to apply. In the early stages of composing an essay (before the actual writing commences), the learner puts together ideas in a fairly random fashion, having adopted a particular stance towards the question, and decided, for example, that *Hamlet* is a tragedy. When the serious business of writing begins, however, the learner is obliged to switch from random thoughts to the strictly linear or sequential technology of pen and paper, and even if notes or an outline for the essay have been prepared carefully, new 'random' thoughts may well supervene, and also the level of concentration tends to drop as the essay progresses. The word processor not only enables 'random' writing of the essay, it also permits the learner to print interim versions of the essay for correction by the tutor and subsequent rewriting.

The results so far obtained indicate that this application has considerable potential; and the only problem I can foresee is the poor learner trying to gain access to the computer, once the teacher discovers the power of the word processor in writing teaching material and books like this one.

(7) Word and number games
Many of the games used in traditional language teaching, together with some newcomers, can be implemented on the micro. Favourite among such games is the ever-popular

'hangman', which exists in a whole variety of variations. In case there is a reader in a far-flung corner of the globe unfamiliar with this game, it consists of an empty gibbet and a series of dashes representing the letters of a word to be guessed by the player. With each unsuccessful attempt, a limb or other part of the body of the unfortunate condemned man is drawn, until either the word is guessed correctly or the man hanged. Ingenious programmers may cause the trap to open and the body to drop. Variations include different levels of difficulty, different subject areas, clues for the learner, and a version for two players.

Computer Scrabble in a foreign language I have yet to see, but a commercial package for Scrabble in English, in which the learner plays the computer, exists and has received reasonable reviews. There should be little difficulty in changing the dictionary on which the game is based to cope with foreign words.

Number games abound; the neatest is the clock game in which either the computer plays one learner, or two play each other. Telling the time in a foreign language often presents problems, and it can be appropriate to isolate the learning of time and present it in the form of a game like this.

There are a number of variations on the theme of 'murder', in which the computer announces that a crime has been committed, and invites the learner to assume the role of detective. One amusing variation draws a picture of the suspect on the screen in accordance with the learner's description of, say, a tall thin woman wearing a hat and carrying a bag. This is a valuable means of associating lexis with visual patterns.

These and other games are a traditional part of language learning, as is the singing of rather dreadful songs, and with colour graphics and appropriate noises from the micro's integral speaker make an attractive additional arm in the weaponry of the teacher, particularly when dealing with less able learners.

(8) Synthetic applications

Artificial intelligence, using machines to act and react in a human fashion, is still a distant goal. It is hard enough to contemplate persuading a computer to adduce general conclusions from specific examples, but the aim of some researchers is to develop 'expert systems', as they are called, which perform like a human teacher, adapting themselves to learner ability and changing performance levels, and improving and modifying their own 'knowledge'.

Such programs are the interest of, among others, Tim Johns of Birmingham Unversity, England, who has written routines which contain rules of morphology – for example, the two forms of the indefinite article in English, 'a' and 'an'. The learner is invited to test the program until it commits an error, in order to explore the limitations of the grammar built into the program. Another kind of synthetic program with an inbuilt grammar is the poetry generator, which is fed a vocabulary and then creates poetry – of a sort – on the screen. Again, the intention is to exploit the learner's curiosity about the general principles – the grammar – on which the program is based.

The best-known synthetic program which incorporates an inbuilt system of its own, in this case an elementary grammar, is called ELIZA, and invites the learner to answer questions, the first of which is 'Tell me your problem.' The program uses its simple grammar to pick out key words from the responses, and a primitive 'dialogue' can be built up. It is also quite fun to change the data of ELIZA to give it (her?) an Oedipus or persecution complex, but such is the very basic level on which it operates that it is clear that sophisticated synthetic programs are a long way off.

All this may come at some time in the future, but for the moment such experiments seem too much like trying to make the computer do something which, in its present form, it is not designed to do. Fifth generation computers may well change all this, but these are still twinkles in the developers' eyes.

The big scare being caused in the West by Japanese research into building 'intelligent computers' which can think like human beings seems as I write now to be a great deal of fuss about misdirected effort. It is surely better to invest effort in realisable goals, such as making computers more accessible to a wider range of users, than to indulge in fashionable research which involves a large measure of crying for the moon. It is as if the lesson of MT in the old days still has not been learned: human discourse is not simply a complex logical code which can be reduced to an algorithm (the statement of a problem in terms of a series of logical steps), it is essentially a human activity which has to do as much with our nature as human beings as with the transmission of meaning.

In my view, it is foolish for CALL practitioners to try themselves to push back the frontiers of computer software design techniques when current CALL itself has yet a very great deal to do in establishing its own ground rules, in fully exploring the areas which have already been recognised as potentially fruitful for CALL, and – not least – in actually writing courseware of sufficient quality and quantity for CALL to become a commonly used and respectable part of language teaching.

(9) **Record and database management systems**

These off-the-peg packages are becoming available for micros but are particularly suited to those machines with large external storage media, such as hard disks. A record or database management system is a means of storing, accessing and analysing information which is usually structured in some way; a bibliography, for example, can be typed into the machine and retrieved in various formats, such as alphabetically sorted by author or in lists of works containing material on a particular aspect of the subject.

Using a micro for such purposes enables the teacher to manage and access his or her resource material far more easily than by other means; but it is important to allow the learner both to access the resource material and also to learn how to use catalogues and similar devices.

These management systems can also be employed in the creation of dictionary-type primary information for the learner.

In the Department of Modern Languages in Dundee we are currently using a record management system to catalogue the holdings of the language laboratory in a far more sophisticated and accessible manner than was hitherto possible. It will now be a relatively simple matter for an EFL student to investigate the database, asking for all the cassette-recorded material on medical topics, or for a student of German to ask for exercises on word order. In addition, it will soon be a straightforward matter to produce selective catalogues as well as a global catalogue in hard copy, by inserting the appropriate typesetting commands into the output files and transmitting them to a computer-driven laser printer which produces camera-ready copy.

(10) General programs

It is more than a little odd that, in all the literature of CALL which has spread through the pages of the computing comics and language journals, there is hardly any reference at all to employing the computer in the advancement of wider language-related skills and to general skills which have particular relevance in language learning.

Let me illustrate what I mean by referring to the problems encountered by learners trying to communicate verbally in a foreign language, particularly under examination conditions. My theory, based on years before the mast as an Advanced Level oral examiner for 18-year-olds, is that those who 'dry up' in French or German and fail to string a few sentences together in answer to a simple question, are not just evidencing a specific weakness in their foreign language acquisition: they are equally inarticulate in their native language, and the problems they are encountering should best be solved at one remove, as it were, from the foreign language. I have suggested to those preparing for oral examinations that they should first question each other in pairs in English before attempting to converse in the language in which they are facing a test.

The language learner is inhibited also by weaknesses in skills which, while not directly concerned with language acquisition, restrict his or her ability to derive the best profit from language learning, and these are skills which are frequently undertaught and seriously underdeveloped even at the undergraduate stage. The most important of these is the ability to read and interpret a catalogue or list of information, and the ability to use dictionary material correctly.

In these general areas the computer can be of very great assistance to the learner – and also to the teacher, if the available resources are catalogued on the computer. This cataloguing can be done by computer in far greater detail and accessed in a much more sophisticated and selective fashion than in manual systems, and the learner profits from employing computer-based systems on a whole variety of different levels, from acquiring familiarity with computers to learning information retrieval skills.

This kind of program is also of great value at a particularly difficult point in the development of the pupil aiming at higher education, at which he or she has to be weaned away in the sixth form from the spoon-feeding of the school educational system to the more self-reliant and learner-directed mode of much university and college education.

The word processor can also be particularly relevant for the learner at this level, in training for note-taking, essay writing, and translation work, as has been described above.

There is a further category of general program which teaches skills that are not directly relevant to language learning, but which either enhance computer awareness (such as typing tutors) or encourage mental dexterity, particularly in relation to coping with a simultaneous range of input from a number of different sources (the flight simulator) or to decision-making skills. This latter type of program typically makes the user the ruler of a country, with a number of factors to cope with, such as the allocation of resources and the interpretation of secret police reports. Where such programs exist in foreign languages, linguistic and general skills can be tested at the same time.

(11) **Real-time control**
The computer can be programmed to control and monitor external devices, such as industrial machinery, robots, and the like. One of the most popular manifestations of external devices controlled by micro is the little wheeled robot which moves about the floor under computer control, drawing graphics on a large sheet of paper. There are two forms of external device which are particularly relevant to language teaching, the videodisc and the computer-controlled cassette recorder, and these are discussed in detail in the next chapter since both represent very new advances in technology, and they add new dimensions – sound and moving pictures – to language learning by computer, exciting possibilities which demand the acquisition of a whole range of new skills by the unfortunate programmer.

From all these varied applications of the computer to CALL, a number of general guidelines and principles emerge, which I now seek to summarise. Like the applications discussed above, these are in no particular order of merit or significance, but attempt to draw together the most obvious positive and negative words of advice to the programmer and user of CALL.

(1) The first concerns the differences, noted above in the case of the EXERCISE package, between dedicated and non-dedicated programs. From the computing point of view, dedicated programs are not exactly cost-effective, since the data and program are bound to one another. As readers will recall from the discussion of the EXERCISE project, it is far more efficient to develop a program which, once written, can operate on a wide variety of

data, not a single set of data as in the letter program. The dividing line, however, between 'dedicated' and 'context-free' programs is never clear cut, since a variety of subroutines created for a dedicated program can be used in other programs; but in some cases very little can be rescued for general use.

(2) Do not be either intimidated by the computer nor carried away by the beginner's enthusiasm. Language teachers are, by virtue of their background and the skills they have learned, peculiarly well adapted to the learning of artificial computer languages, better adapted (dare I say) than many scientists who may master the technicalities more swiftly because of their background in electronics, but who lack the 'feel' for languages. On the other side of the coin, it is fatal to write a ten-line program in some vestigial subset of BASIC, and then compound the felony by proclaiming the fact to the educational world at large. The computing press and, regrettably, academic journals too, are filled with articles by computing neophytes who, on mature reflection, must be crawling with embarrassment at their first fumbling steps in a very complex area of human knowledge. I have a couple of such efforts to my own discredit which I would wish long dead and buried without trace.

(3) Do not be afraid to experiment. The ground rules are still being written, and even the relative beginner with some flair for computing (and flair is essential, just like in playing a musical instrument) will discover new ways of presenting material and new approaches to programming. Always conduct field tests on learners: they will crash your program in no time in ways that you did not think were possible. Always try a program designed for a university undergraduate out on a nine-year-old first.

(4) In all these applications, it is critical that the appearance of the text on the screen causes no additional problems to the learner: accents and other diacritical marks should appear without resort to second best, such as *e1* for *é*,

and so forth. In the earlier days of computing, when the character set was fixed and attuned to scientific applications, this was a tall order indeed; nowadays, however, this presents no problems. Modern micros either have switchable ROM character sets, or software user-definable characters, which can cope with most of the difficulties presented by different languages, cyrillic and more exotic still included. Some of the authoring packages can also accept user-defined character sets. The only difficulty is that of definition: on the 8 × 8 matrix which is all that the BBC micro allows for character definition, capital A with diaeresis or circumflex accent is hardly clear. However, there is a way round this difficulty: by employing the facility on the BBC micro to fuse the graphics and text cursors, it is possible to type the text and then draw in the accents in a far clearer way than is possible with the character set facility.

(5) Careful design of the appearance of material on the screen is essential. Some of the earlier efforts on now outdated micro systems had a distinct air of amateurishness, and there is now no excuse for failing to exploit the full potential of the micro for attractive layout and, where possible, colour. In addition, there ought to be an international ban on the hitherto ubiquitous BASIC question-mark prompt, which should be able to be suppressed on any serious system.

(6) Matching input with the model answer, which forms the basis of the simplest kind of CALL, should be applied with great care. This does not only apply to situations in which the learner accidentally hits the shift key on the micro (unless the shift key can be set by the micro itself) or types superfluous spaces or punctuation in a response, but particularly to the concept of 'wild cards' referred to earlier, in which an asterisk or question mark can stand for one or more characters. One cautionary tale refers to preventing learners in Scottish schools from typing rude words in their responses to the

letter-creating program, and '*ERDE' caused the computer to react somewhat unfavourably. The results for those who wrote, quite innocently, 'J'habite à Aberdeen', were unfortunate in the least.

(7) Consider the longer-term problems of portability of programs. One of the inevitable results of free enterprise in the field of computing is that there is a multiplicity of different computers, operating systems, programming languages, and the like, all vying for attention and all claiming to be the industry standard, and it is an additional burden for the beginner to have to decide which machine to learn on if hard-won skills are not to be prejudiced by out-of-date or unpopular hardware. In many cases, these decisions are made by the holders of purse strings at some remote centre, but portability (machine independence) is a key issue for those programs which have a general applicability.

(8) Let the computer do what it can do well. Do not try to redefine the limits of computing applicability; these will inevitably extend over the coming decades, but the present situation is such that the technology has once more outstripped our ability to use it properly, and those areas well within the current capabilities of the computer have yet to be fully explored by researchers in the field.

(9) The computer should be integrated into the teaching process, not become a separate and unrelated activity. Not least because its strengths are highly specific, the micro is at its best as part of an overall teaching strategy. One of the most effective ways to integrate the micro is to use it as an extension of existing school or university courses. This is being done in some Scottish schools with the 'Tour de France' French course to good effect.

(10) The role of the computer should not be seen specifically as that of teacher or tester of aspects of the language being learnt. Its role as an information storage and retrieval device and especially as a means for the

strengthening of general skills should not be underestimated, nor should its potential as an examining (and marking!) device. It is quite easy to adapt a homemade package (and at least one commercially available package) to a testing mode, in which the computer assumes the role of examiner, and can record the marks of the learner. Progress has yet to be made on a program to write the appropriate report entries for the pupils concerned! A related issue is that of the potential of the computer as a teacher of new material. Most of the material currently on offer reinforces rather than teaches, although there are commercially available packages for elementary foreign language teaching from Atari and Wida Software, for example. More attention has yet to be given to designing packages which extend the knowledge of the learner in particular areas of language acquisition.

(11) Careful consideration should be given to the kinds of learner who are offered micro tuition, since much of the available CALL material is clearly designed to serve a remedial function. By 'careful consideration' I mean that there are two distinct schools of thought in relation to the role of the micro in helping the remedial learner. One side takes the view that the micro is an ideal machine for the backward pupil, the other takes the view that it is undesirable to separate out any kind of pupil (whether remedial or extra bright) from the generality of the class. In addition, it has been pointed out more than once that, in CALL as in so many other areas of education, an excess of emphasis has been placed on the very bright and the very dull learner; but the poor average learner, who happens to be in the large majority, has had far less than his or her due share of attention.

(12) A correct balance must be maintained in the flow of information to the learner. The screen should not be crowded with information, nor should colour be used to

excess. Questions of legibility and the extent to which information presented on the screen is retained have still to be resolved; this is, like so much in CALL, a relatively new area. But it does seem that the old general educational principle still holds good on the TV screen: Say what you are going to say, say it, and then say you've said it. In other words, material should be properly introduced, then discussed and tested where appropriate, and rounded off by a summary.

(13) Software must satisfy certain minimum requirements. In the first place, it must not get in between the learner and the subject. There are some horrendous examples of how not to write software around, but, to spare the guilty, I offer some invented examples by way of illustration. Let us assume the package is one which asks a series of questions. There is little point in posing the question 'What is the French for strike?' if the context does not make clear what kind of strike is being asked for, a withdrawal of labour or something that should be done while the iron is hot. Equally ludicrous is the situation in which the package asks 'What is the German for hyperbolic paraboloid?' and obstinately refuses to accept an answer without the definite article in front of it, unless of course the learner has been warned that the article is essential.

Equally unpardonable is the program which does not explain to the learner why an answer is wrong, but simply says 'Correct' or 'Incorrect. The correct answer is . . .' Reinforcement does not have to take place immediately; if learner responses are monitored, as was the case with the EXERCISE package, errors and their correction can be discussed by the learners in a group under the guidance of their teacher.

A practical point overlooked by far too many writers of CALL material is the fact that the keyboard should be made proof against accidental or deliberate sabotage by the user. Most micros will have a key marked

'Escape' and another marked 'Break', both of which normally interrupt the running of a program, the latter with more finality than the former. These keys should be disabled by the program. In addition, most micros have a buffered keyboard, that is, it is possible to type ahead of what appears on the screen. This can be disastrous if a menu is about to come up on the screen and the learner has to decide among several options; the buffering of the keyboard should be disabled, as also should the repeat facility, which causes the same character to be repeated on the screen after an interval if the user holds a key down.

Another undesirable quality in CALL programs, usually those written by the newly-converted enthusiast, is the programmer's very enthusiasm, which tends to run out of control and create unfortunate results on the screen. When I first discovered how easy it was to program colour text and graphics in Teletext mode on the BBC Micro, the results oscillated between the bilious and the psychedelic. Others who discovered the effectiveness of graphics have found that their delight in creating figures which dismember themselves horribly if the learner gets the wrong answer has led to learners deliberately opting for the incorrect response.

(14) An appropriate balance must be maintained between effort and reward. It will be recalled from my first efforts with the EXERCISE package that the length of the exercises was excessive: CALL is a very intense activity, and requires the dedicated concentration of the learner. It is advisable to break up the time spent at the micro (which itself should not be excessively long – I suspect 20 minutes is the maximum before counter-productivity sets in) into very small units, in which the learner is appropriately reinforced, marked out of a total, or is in some way complimented if the performance is good, or pointed in the direction of remedial assistance if that is required.

(15) CALL represents a welcome shift towards learner-directed instruction; but this mode of learning does have inbuilt demerits which should be coped with in the design of CALL software. The most significant of these is the fact that learners, with their worm's eye view of the subject they are seeking to acquire, are not always in the best position to determine why they have made errors, what the most appropriate remedial action is, or what the next step in the learning process should be.

(16) When the language laboratory came on the scene, and for some time thereafter, many considered that it was suited only to beginners, not to the more advanced learner. The same myth has attached itself to CALL, and it is hoped that some of the material in this chapter, notably the section on the word processor, has exploded this myth. CALL can be applied across the whole range of language acquisition and related skills.

(17) It is not necessary for everyone interested in employing the micro to become an expert programmer, but it is essential to become sufficiently familiar with what the micro can and cannot do if you are to apply it in the classroom. This knowledge does not have to be at a particularly high level; in fact, this book should have given you enough insight to be able to understand the potential and limitations of the micro, and to know if any ideas you have can profitably be adapted for the micro.

(18) Above all, do not ignore the micro, even if it is not attractive to you after all the persuasive words in this book. It cannot be persuaded to go away simply by pretending it does not exist.

8

Linking the micro to other devices

There are many pieces of electrical equipment to which the micro can be linked, and in what follows I shall discuss the most important of them; it must, however, not be forgotten that the micro can and should be linked to devices other than the purely electrical. Not the least of these is the humble book. The coursebook with a floppy disk in the back is just over the horizon, and stresses the chief role of CALL as a supplement to rather than a replacement for personal teaching.

The computer can readily be applied to real-time control of external devices (a robot making Italian cars is a dedicated computer controlling a machine), and there are a number of external devices which can be adapted for CALL use.

(1) Intelligent tape recorder

Research work has been in progress for some time in two centres at least on applying a random-access tape recorder to computer-assisted learning: in the Chemistry Department at Wolverhampton Polytechnic under Keith Miller, and at the University of Dundee under myself. The Wolverhampton project concentrates on the recorder itself, whilst I have been developing programs in which the recorder is driven by a separate microcomputer with a screen.

The concept is as follows: tape is a linear device, and, given the usual mechanical counter on a tape recorder, particularly a cassette machine, it is not possible to locate material with pinpoint accuracy, and certainly not under automatic external control. Imagine, however, a situation in which a cassette recorder can be placed under the control of a microcomputer which can not only determine and monitor all the functions of the recorder (wind, play, record, stop, and so on), but can also be persuaded to wind to, stop at, and record or play from predetermined locations on the tape with an accuracy of plus or minus 0.5 second.

The first experiments in these projects, undertaken with hardware developed largely by Tandberg Ltd, involved a conventional language laboratory tape recorder (which can work on both tracks simultaneously: one is called the master track, on which model material is placed, and which can only be listened to by the learner, and the other the student track, on to which the learner records his or her response). The master track was used for recording tone bursts which could be detected by the microcomputer. One of two techniques could be adopted: either the tone bursts could be at regular, predetermined frequencies, or they could be written to the tape as and when required by the creator of courseware. This method presented a number of quite difficult technical problems, not the least of which was the ability to keep the tape in contact with the read head whilst winding, so that the tone bursts could be counted, and this approach was finally abandoned when a new tape recorder was developed which had its own microprocessor.

This machine has an on-board software digital clock, which is a jargon-ridden way of saying that, instead of a mechanical tape counter, it has a digital read-out (rather like that familiar from digital watches with a stop-watch facility), which can be zeroised at the beginning of the tape. The read-out relates to the tape in terms of minutes and seconds from the beginning of the tape. This digital display is generated by a microprocessor, and all the keys on the recorder are under microprocessor control, preventing, for example, the user from ejecting the tape whilst rewinding or recording. These computer control functions were initially designed for incorporating the recorder into a microprocessor-controlled language laboratory, but are now being adapted to direct control from a microcomputer.

Let us take by way of illustration of the way in which this hardware can be applied to CALL the first project being developed in Dundee, namely, the automation of the dictation and related exercises.

The normal pattern for a dictation exercise (the object of which is to test the learner's ability to hear and understand a foreign language text, and then to write down the material heard as accurately as possible) is that the teacher reads the text through once at normal pace, whilst the learner listens. A second read-through is conducted at a slower speed, with pauses after every two or three words and indications of punctuation marks, during which the learner writes down his or her version of the text. A third and final read-through enables the learner to check through this version and make corrections, after which the dictation is collected by the teacher, marked, and comments on errors made are communicated to the learner.

It is a mechanical exercise which is, in the right circumstances, invaluable to the learner, but which consumes a great deal of contact time which might more productively be used in different ways; in addition, some learners need much more practice in this work than others. In other words, this kind of exercise is an ideal candidate for computerisation (to use a nasty neologism), and, given the right hardware, presents relatively few programming problems whilst at the same time creating a powerful learning tool.

There is an important additional advantage closely related to the procedure discussed in the previous chapter in the matter of compositional skills. The exercise is no longer one which almost invariably falls into two distinct phases, of (1) the learner producing one final version and (2) the teacher correcting and commenting on that version. Given the potential and flexibility of the computer, it is quite feasible – and indeed desirable – to permit the learner to seek to improve on his or her response to the dictation, once it has been marked on the screen; according to conditions which can either be set by the teacher or the learner, the latter may attempt to make further corrections with or without hearing the dictation through a further time or times. In addition, the interaction between learner and computer is instantaneous; the marked version appears immediately and accurately on the screen, not a couple of days later from the teacher.

The computer version of the dictation goes something like this. First, on the screen appears the title of the dictation together with an audio message confirming that the learner has (or has not!) got the right match of tape and disk. At this and subsequent stages, the learner unfamiliar with the system is invited to ask for help as to what the procedure is, how to type and correct responses on the screen, and so forth. Second, the learner is given the first read-through of the text to be tested, during which time he or she simply listens.

The next stage is that of the second read-through of the passage. This time it is divided up into small sections, each of which, where possible, is a sense unit of some kind, and with each of which punctuation marks are given on the audio tape. After each section, the tape pauses until the learner has typed in a version of that section and has indicated by hitting the return key that he or she has finished. At this stage, the learner is permitted to delete characters or delete the whole line and start again.

After the conclusion of this stage, the text is read through one more time, during which the learner compares his or her written version with the spoken word. Then the learner is permitted to edit this version. The amount of editing allowed can be varied under program control.

Once the editing has been completed, the learner's version is marked on the screen by the following method: an arrow is placed under the first incorrect character in any given line and the total number of errors indicated. At this point, again at the discretion of the programmer, further attempts at editing or listening to part or all of the passage are permitted.

The final stage of the procedure is the facility for the inclusion by the programmer of visual and/or audio comments on the dictation, in particular on certain errors flagged in advance. For example, if a common pitfall is the typing of 'j'avais' with a final 't' instead of 's', and this cluster appears on line two, the programmer can set up the dictation in such a way that a visual comment plus an audio reinforcement can be given if the learner makes this error.

Then the learner can be informed of which dictation to do next, if he or she wishes to do further work, and enforced branching to a back-up exercise can also be incorporated.

The procedure for the teacher who may or may not know anything about computing, and who wishes to set up a suite of dictations, is made as simple as possible. The text of the dictation is recorded by the teacher, who leaves gaps of roughly five seconds' silence between each small section of the text. The exact length of time does not matter, as long as it exceeds three seconds. The audio cassette created should leave a gap of, say, one minute's play time before the dictation begins, for reasons which will become clear in a moment. The cassette is placed in the recorder, which is linked to the computer. A program is run which works out where the parts of the dictation are on the tape, using a combination of two instructions. The first tells the recorder to play until three seconds' silence is encountered; the second reads the digital clock time from the recorder. (This is just an outline description of a procedure which, for the programmer, is a little more complicated that that.) Having worked out the location of the various parts of the dictation, the computer rewinds the recorder, and stores in digital form the block structure of the tape on the beginning of the tape itself.

The above utility program can be applied to the extended version of the TES/T package, and indeed to other programs written independently by the user, and is designed to make the location of audio information on the tape a very simple procedure for the user.

(2) **Videodisc**

Linking the micro to some form of video equipment has the distinct advantage of bringing into the learning situation pictorial images from the real world – not graphics, however skilful, but actual people in actual situations. Unfortunately, the currently most popular recording medium for video, the videocassette, is not particularly well suited to any but the most primitive and undemanding CALL applications, because of the slow access time and the general inability to produce clear frozen frames.

At the time of writing, the whole future of the commercial videodisc industry is in considerable doubt, and, as stated earlier in relation to computers and computer-related hardware, it is only when a product finds a strong, widely-based commercial or home market that it can be readily (and not too expensively) applied and adapted to educational use.

The videocassette dominates this market, but has little to offer to CALL, since it is a linear storage device with very poor access times and no pinpoint accuracy of frame location. The videodisc recorder, if and when it penetrates into the market place, has two vital attributes. It is a random-access device; the read head can scan from one end of the disk to the other very swiftly indeed (the worst case being in the region of five seconds) and with guaranteed precision, enabling information (TV frames, text, programs, or data) to be accessed under computer control. Secondly, it can store huge amounts of information: one typical disk can hold (it has been calculated) the entire *Encyclopedia Britannica* four times over on one side.

If to those two qualities a third could be added, the videodisc would present an impressive new quantum leap forward, not just for CALL, but for a vast range of computer applications. This quality is the ability to write information on to the disk; the readily available hardware at present allows only reading of information, but there is a promise of such developments in the near future. If and when this materialises, a whole new world of information technology will be opened up. At present it is possible to superimpose teletext characters (such as are used in Ceefax and Oracle) generated from a computer, hence incorporating CALL into off-the-shelf material. Given a videodisc full of stills or moving sequences from everyday French life, an impressive package of material could be built up with relative ease.

Imagine a situation in which it is possible to present text, images and sound to the learner, and to capture the learner's spoken response on cassette. One such, which must be at one and the same time the most imaginative and most awfully titled project so far undertaken, rejoices under the name of Montevidisco and was developed at Brigham Young University, USA, for the teaching of Spanish.

The student is shown the plaza in the centre of a town, and is asked questions, invited to respond, and can repeat sequences or take up different options. A detailed account of this package is to be found in the first issue of CALICO (see the Bibliographical Appendix).

(3) Speech synthesis and voice recognition

These two, as far as the language teacher is concerned, are still a long way off, except for the use of the former for giving audio instructions to the learner.

9

Conclusion

It seems somewhat inappropriate to end this book with a conclusion, since what I have been seeking to describe is really only a beginning on the long road to what I believe to be a secure and positive role for the computer in many aspects of language teaching in the future. It does seem appropriate, however, to try and reach an interim conclusion by drawing up something of a credit and debit balance of computing in language teaching as it stands at the moment.

Many of the supposed demerits of the computer are really nothing of the sort. Take for example the criticism I have heard of some software that it has been presented in a boring and unimaginative fashion: that is a criticism not of the computer, but of the bad workman on the machine. In addition, critics have rightly called attention to programs which do little more than transfer tedious drills from another medium, the book. Again, lack of imagination and the inability to adopt new techniques appropriate to the new medium are to blame, not the computer itself. I am reminded of the delightful *Punch* cartoon from the early days of television in the classroom. A teacher is berating an unfortunate child with these words: 'How dare you do homework when you should be watching television!'

Here in summary are the merits and demerits of CALL, the merits first.

(1) CALL is sensitive to the needs of the individual learner. Group teaching always comes up against the intractable problems of variable rates of learning (not just between

one individual and another, but with the same individual at different levels and kinds of skill). As a result CALL can be used for remedial work. CALL can also increase the degree of interaction between learner and teacher, whether the mechanical 'teacher' or the human teacher – as in the examples of dictation and composition exercises cited above.

(2) The response from CALL is instant; instead of the work gathering dust in the staffroom until the teacher gets round to correcting it, the learner gains from an immediate response together with reinforcing commentary. The absence of a time-lag improves the learning rate and maintains a high level of motivation.

(3) CALL is not only interactive in the sense of dialogue between computer and learner, but also in that it is possible actually to increase the dialogue between learner and teacher. Instead of a piece of work being done in an exercise book and handed to the teacher for marking, a gradualist approach can be adopted, as was seen above in the case of the essay skills program. The learner can break down the task into smaller, more manageable units, and what was once irrevocably committed to paper in final form, can now be submitted in draft and revised according to the suggestions of the teacher.

(4) CALL can increase the quality of communication between teacher and learner: out of a class of thirty or so, there will be at least a handful of learners, however good the teacher, who will fail fully to understand new material presented during class. CALL material can be accessed by learners in difficulty as often as necessary, and at the pace which suits the individual learner.

(5) CALL encourages open knowledge, not just of the computer, but of the subject being learned. The new technology is not a threat, but a challenge. Only those with closed minds need fear it. The humanities have always been at the heart of our educational system, and there is no threat posed in the foreseeable future by the

computer. The core of the humanities is not computeris-
able: morality, art, and culture are not yet within the
grasp of the machine. In the hierarchy of wisdom,
knowledge, information, computers are firmly in the
third category.

(6) CALL increases computer literacy on the part of the
learner in an age when the explosion in information
technology is just getting into gear.

(7) One of the great advantages of the micro, which is not
directly linked to language teaching, is the fact that it
is not like a language laboratory or a tape-slide synchro-
niser or any of the other hardware of educational technology: its applications do not cease within the narrow
context of CALL work. The micro can be used to keep
class records, maintain financial accounts, produce and
hold copies of class notes and bibliographies, which can
be updated with great ease – in fact there is a host of
'peripheral' applications which not only aid the language
teacher's work, but which can be justifiably employed as
arguments for the acquisition of a micro in the face of
possibly uncomprehending opposition from outsiders
who hold the purse strings for equipment purchase.

By contrast, the list of demerits is relatively short.

(1) It is difficult to apply CALL to deductive reasoning, to
deducing rules from examples.

(2) There is also the danger of researchers in the field failing
to cooperate, but this is not likely in the UK. There must
be a coordinated effort to enable those who are pushing
back the frontiers of knowledge to work in a collabora-
tive, mutually informed manner. This is happening in the
UK with help of CILT and CALLBOARD (see Bibliographical Appendix).

Having said all this about CALL, in the last analysis modern
language teaching more than any other discipline depends not
on technology or methodology, but on the qualities and

personality of the individual teacher. I can only hope that the best of the profession will at least give CALL a chance.

Do not be too hasty to praise or condemn CALL: it is, for the linguist, a comparatively new tool, and one which has emerged at a time of rapidly developing technology. Without experimentation by the hardy few and sensible sitting on the fence by the not-so-hardy many, this tool will never be allowed the breathing space to develop whatever potential it may possess. The cynic should not condemn CALL out of hand for not yet being a perfected tool: it will take some years for suitable courseware to emerge, and even longer – if ever – for computer courseware to be as common a phenomenon as a school textbook; after all, good quality material did not spring instantaneously out of the language laboratory or television when they were invented.

On a broader canvas, computer awareness is an essential part of the child's educational experience, and nothing but good can come from extending the role of the computer into the language teaching area of the curriculum. Further, neither teacher nor learner can cosily assume, as in the past, that the educational process is like climbing a single ladder, at the top of which the learner emerges, clutching a certificate, education finished for good and all. In a rapidly changing technological world, all that can be said about the future with certainty is that it is uncertain. Not only will education increasingly be a lifelong process, with the need to learn new skills and discard old ones; it will also no longer be linear and hierarchical but a multifaceted experience, branching not just upwards, but outwards into a whole number of unexpected avenues. And, I suspect, wherever the twists and turns of education in the future lead, there will be a computer involved somewhere. Educationalists, even language teachers, will ignore the computer, like it or not, at their peril.

Bibliographical appendix

Books

G. Davies and J. J. Higgins, *Computers, Language and Language Learning*, CILT Information Guide no. 22, London, 1982. (This is an excellent factual study of CALL and required reading for anyone seeking a clear state-of-the-art account and a sound bibliography. A new updated edition is planned for late 1984.)

J. R. Hartley, 'Computer Assisted Learning,' in: H. T. Smith and T. R. G. Green (eds.), *Human Interaction with Computers*, London, 1980, pp. 129-159. (The best account of the theoretical issues of CAL available.)

J. J. Higgins and T. Johns, *Computers in Language Learning*, London and Glasgow, 1984.

S. M. Hockey, *A Guide to Computer Applications in the Humanities*, London, 1980. (This is a lucid and intelligently written survey of the material I discuss in Chapter 2, although it is now somewhat out of date.)

M. J. Kenning and M.-M. Kenning, *Introduction to Computer Assisted Language Teaching*, Oxford 1983.

Journals
ALLC Journal and ALLC Bulletin
ALLC Secretary

Department of English
University College of North Wales
Bangor
Wales
(Publications of the Association for Literary and Linguistic
Computing, a world-wide organisation of academics.)

CAL News, CET (See addresses below) (A broadsheet giving
up-to-date information on all aspects of CAL.)

CALICO Journal
229 KMB
Brigham Young University
Provo
Utah 84602
USA
(The title is an acronym for Computer Assisted Language
Learning and Instruction Consortium. Many useful articles
on languages and the computer, especially on TICCIT and
videodisc.)

CALLBOARD
19 High St
Eccleshall
Stafford ST21 6BW
(An information sheet on research into computers and
modern languages.)

Educational Computing
Alan Wells International Ltd.
P.O. Box 50
Farndon Rd
Market Harborough
Leics
(A monthly glossy covering the whole range of computers in
schools, with frequent references to modern languages.)

Videodisc Newsletter
University of London Audio-Visual Centre
North Wing Studios
Senate House
Malet St
London WC1E 7JZ
(Broadsheet giving information on interactive videodisc in all areas of education.)

Addresses
CET (Council for Educational Technology)
3 Devonshire St
London W1N 2BA

CILT (Centre for Information on Language Teaching and Research) 20 Carlton House Terrace
London
SW1Y 5AP
(CILT produces a bibliography of Computer-Based Learning, and holds a directory of research in the field.)

Software producers
(I make reference to several of the following in some detail in the text.)
CAMSOFT
10 Wheatfield Close
Maidenhead
Berks
SL6 3PS
(Questionmaster is available from this producer.)

KOSMOS Software
1 Pilgrims Close
Harlington
Dunstable
LU5 6LX

(Produce programs on cassette for French, German and Spanish for BBC B and Spectrum 48K.)

LocheeSoft
5 Inverary Terrace
Dundee
DD3 6BS
(Produce the French Pronouns Program, German Sentence Building and Context, a gapping program.)

Tandberg Ltd
Unit 1
Revie Rd
Elland Rd
Leeds
LS11 8JG
(Produce the TES/T package with or without AECAL extension for the BBC B. A dictation package for BBC B and AECAL recorder is also available.)

Wida Software
2 Nicholas Gardens
London
W5 5HY
(Produce, for Apple only, Apfeldeutsch, an ambitious ab initio course, and German routines for the BBC and other machines.)

Index